praise for the nationally bestselling
life in motion: an unlikely ballerina
(Atria 2014)

"Wrenching and revelatory."
—*The New York Times*

"[A] dramatic rags-to-toe-shoes life story."
—*People*

☆ "An unexpected page turner . . . Her story is an inspiration to anyone—man or woman, black or white—who has ever chased a dream against the odds, and the grace with which she triumphs is an example for us all."
—*Booklist* (starred review)

"A raw, honest tale of growing up and into the calling of a lifetime. . . . Her memoir is filled with passion, pain, success, and . . . pure joy."
—*Ebony*

also by misty copeland

Firebird

life in motion

motion

an unlikely ballerina

young readers edition

MISTY COPELAND

with Brandy Colbert

Aladdin

NEW YORK   LONDON   TORONTO   SYDNEY   NEW DELHI

ALADDIN

An imprint of Simon & Schuster Children's Publishing Division

1230 Avenue of the Americas, New York, New York 10020

First Aladdin hardcover edition December 2016

For information about special discounts for bulk purchases, please contact
Simon & Schuster Special Sales at 1-866-506-1949 or business@simonandschuster.com.

The Simon & Schuster Speakers Bureau can bring authors to your live event.
For more information or to book an event contact the Simon & Schuster Speakers Bureau
at 1-866-248-3049 or visit our website at www.simonspeakers.com.

Jacket designed by Dan Potash

Interior designed by Mike Rosamilia

The text of this book was set in Adobe Garamond Pro.

Manufactured in the United States of America 0117 FFG

4 6 8 10 9 7 5 3

Library of Congress Cataloging-in-Publication Data

Names: Copeland, Misty, author. | Colbert, Brandy.

Title: Life in motion : an unlikely ballerina / by Misty Copeland with Brandy Colbert

Aladdin.

Description: Young Readers edition. | New York : Aladdin, 2016. |

Includes bibliographical references and index.

Identifiers: LCCN 2016036841 | ISBN 9781481479790 (hardcover : alk. paper)

Subjects: LCSH: Copeland, Misty. | Ballet dancers—United States—Biography. |

Ballerinas—United States—Biography. | African American

dancers—Biography.

Classification: LCC GV1785.C635 C66 2016 | DDC 792.8092 [B]—dc23

LC record available at https://lccn.loc.gov/2016036841

ISBN 9781481479813 (eBook)

Insert photos: p. 3, top: Rosalie O'Connor; p. 6: Getty Images;
p. 7, top (inset): Marcia E. Wilson; with Herman Cornejo: Gene Schiavone;
p. 8: Rosalie O'Connor. All other photos from the author's personal collection.

To all ballerinas and dancers of the world.

Our art is vital.

Let's keep it alive, growing, and expanding!

chapter 1

FOR AS LONG AS I CAN REMEMBER, I'VE LED A
life in motion.

When I was two years old, I rode a bus from Kansas
City, Missouri, to our new home in Southern California.
I was the youngest back then, with two older brothers,
Doug and Chris, and an older sister named Erica. Mommy
moved us away from our father to a sunny suburb of Los
Angeles called Bellflower, where we would live with her
new husband, Harold.

I don't remember the bus ride, but when I think back
to those years, I always remember my time with Harold.
He liked jokes and he had a great laugh, one that would
make everyone around him laugh too. My baby sister,

Lindsey, was born after we'd lived with Harold for three years, so I wasn't the youngest anymore. But even with five of us kids to look after, Harold would find time to spend alone with each of us. I loved when I'd sit on the couch with him, eating sunflower seeds.

But when I was seven, Mommy decided we needed to leave our home again. Without Harold. And Lindsey was coming with us. This was the second time Mommy had packed us up and moved us to a new place, and we didn't know why. We loved Harold. Later, she would tell us he drank too much. He was an alcoholic. He mostly hid it from me and my brothers and sisters. But when I remember Harold, I don't think of the beer cans that always sat on the nightstand he shared with Mommy. I remember how kind he was and how he made waffles for Lindsey and me on Saturday mornings while we watched cartoons.

This time we moved only about twenty miles away, to a community in Los Angeles called San Pedro. Even though we were in a big city, San Pedro felt like a storybook town, where we had bonfires on the beach and took school field trips to a lighthouse. Part of the Port of Los Angeles is located in San Pedro, where goods like furniture, clothes, and car parts are shipped in.

Our new house was close to the Pacific Ocean, with a big front yard and a view of Catalina Island. It also had a new stepfather, named Robert. We missed Harold, and it didn't take long to notice the differences between Mommy's old husband and her new one. Robert was stricter. He made us do chores around the house, and we ate breakfast, lunch, and dinner at the dining room table instead of on the couch in front of the TV.

Robert called me "little Hawaiian girl" and said I looked like his family. Like me, he was of mixed ancestry. His family had roots in Hawaii, Korea, the Philippines, Portugal, and Japan. Mommy had been adopted by an African American couple, but her biological parents were Italian and black. Our father, whom we left in Missouri, was also biracial, with a black father and a German mother.

I guess I did look a bit more like Robert's family than my brothers and sisters, but I didn't think about that when we were together. I loved them, and we were a united force. Still, the way I looked mattered to Robert, and especially to his family. Everyone knew I was Robert's favorite, and soon it became clear that his family felt the same way. I went over to his parents' house in the summer, where Grandma Marie taught me how to sew clothing for my dolls. But

Doug, Chris, Erica, and Lindsey almost never came with me. And Robert's father, Grandpa Martin, would hide in his bedroom when all of us visited. I don't remember him ever speaking to me or my brothers and sisters.

Robert was strict about us kids helping clean up around the house. We would get in trouble if we didn't follow his rules. He made us stand in the corner without talking. Doug and Chris were punished more often than us girls, though. They'd have to stare at the wall for at least an hour, and sometimes Robert would make them stand completely still as they balanced a thick book on their heads. I didn't like when they were being disciplined, especially when Robert was particularly mean. Like when he dragged Chris across the house by his ear. Or worse, when Robert got so mad that he hit Chris with a frying pan.

But he didn't stop there. When Chris and Doug would argue with each other, Robert made them work it out by boxing in the backyard. "Since you guys can't agree, you'll have to fight it out," he would say.

We all became so scared of him that we tried our best to make sure the house was always in perfect order when he was home. We avoided him as much as we could. My big sister, Erica, slept over at her friend's house, and I would spend a lot of time with Doug and Chris in the room they shared, listening to music by our favorite hip-hop groups. But no matter how hard we tried to stay out of his way, Robert would find a reason to be mad at us. And he was almost always mad at our baby sister.

Lindsey resembled her father, Harold, and her African features were more pronounced than the rest of ours. Robert didn't like this, and he blamed her for everything. I was shocked the first time I heard him call her the N word. But soon the slur would flow so freely from his mouth that none of us were surprised.

Mommy was scared of Robert, too. She'd complain about him when he wasn't around, but when he was being terrible to us, she wouldn't say anything. She didn't shield us from him, but she didn't protect herself, either. After a while, our mother couldn't hide the bruises Robert would leave on her skin.

Mommy's adoptive parents had given her a good home, but she was still young when they'd died. She'd had a hard childhood, moving a lot to stay with different family members. Sometimes we wondered if that's why she moved us around so much.

One day, after we'd been living with Robert for about

four years, Mommy told us we were leaving him forever. "We've got to get out of here," she said, so scared that she whispered even when he wasn't around. "Robert can't have a hint that we're leaving. When it's time, I'll let you know."

Knowing that we were leaving him soon made it easier to deal with Robert's anger and unpredictable moods. And then, one day, it was time to go. Robert left for work in the morning, like usual, but instead of leaving for her job, our mother stayed home. She flung open the door to the room I shared with Erica and said, "Today's the day."

By that time, we had a baby brother, Cameron, Mommy's son with Robert. We all rushed around the house, cramming our suitcases with as many of our belongings as would fit. A strange car pulled up to the house then, driven by a man we didn't know. He didn't look anything like Robert. He was a tall white man with brown hair and glasses.

We quickly learned he was there to help, and he began loading our bags into his car. Mommy told us his name was Ray. He was our mother's new boyfriend.

chapter 2

AFTER WE LEFT ROBERT, WE BRIEFLY STAYED with Mommy's friends in downtown L.A. They were Auntie Monique and Uncle Charles to my siblings and me.

They were kind to us, but their neighborhood was home to gang activity. I didn't feel safe living there. If any of us wore a color the gang didn't like, I knew something bad could happen.

Then, one night, we heard gunshots outside. There was a loud *thump*, like something heavy had landed on the front porch. When we ran outside, a man was lying there. Blood from where a bullet had hit him bloomed into a bigger and bigger circle on his jeans.

We moved a few weeks after that. I was happy to get away from the drive-by shootings and gangs in Auntie Monique and Uncle Charles's neighborhood. But my good mood didn't last. Not once I found out we'd be living with Ray.

We were annoyed that our mother always seemed to need a boyfriend or a husband. We wanted to stop moving around so much. We wanted a mother who wouldn't make us live with dangerous people, like Robert, or in dangerous areas, like with Auntie Monique and Uncle Charles. We wanted her to feel like she didn't need anybody but us.

Mommy worked in sales, and her income was unpredictable. Ray didn't make a lot at his job, either, so the eight of us had to live on very little money. We mostly ate packaged food, like potato chips and ramen noodles. Sometimes we'd have a can of vegetables to round it out. Our mother didn't cook much, but she would give money to my older siblings to buy groceries. My brother Chris, who had learned how to cook from Robert, would prepare our meals.

We didn't like Ray. He was nerdy. He tried too hard to make us like him. And our mother changed when she was around him. They got matching tattoos, and she kissed him in front of us like they were teenagers.

We only had to put up with Ray for about a year, because soon Mommy had a new boyfriend: Alex. We moved into his apartment. Like Ray's, it was tiny, and the six of us kids slept on the living room floor, leaving the bedroom to Mommy and Alex. Mommy lost her job and then our car. After a while, Alex was kicked out of his apartment and we had to move again—to a motel.

Alex came with us to the Sunset Inn, and again we were living in a cramped space. But soon Cameron would leave us. His father, Robert, took our mother to court and got primary custody. That meant Cameron lived with us only on the weekends. I cried and cried when he left. He was the baby in the family, and even though we were all young, it felt like we'd helped Mommy raise him.

Cameron moving out seemed like the thread that started to unravel our family. Erica was spending the night with friends more often than she stayed at home, and Lindsey spent several weeks with her father, Harold. Money was so tight that sometimes we'd search through the couch cushions and carpet for loose change, hoping to come up with enough to buy food at the corner store. After it became clear she could no longer support us, Mommy applied for food stamps.

I didn't want anyone at school to know about our situation, so I pretended everything was fine. I didn't have friends over, instead choosing to go to their homes so they wouldn't have to see the crowded motel room I shared with my family. I didn't want them to know my meals consisted of the food I could afford in the vending machines of the motel hallway.

But I couldn't hide where I lived forever.

chapter 3

THE FIRST TIME I STEPPED ONSTAGE WASN'T
for a ballet recital—it was for the talent show at Thomas
Jefferson Elementary School in Bellflower, California.

I was five years old and I was going to lip-synch and
dance to a song called "Please Mr. Postman" with Erica and
Chris. Mommy helped us prepare, sewing our costumes
and watching us practice in the living room after school.

The night of the talent show, my sister and I danced and
mouthed the lyrics while Chris played a postal worker, sending envelopes sailing into the crowd from his fake mailbag.
Everyone loved the performance, especially our mother. "You
guys were great!" she said, excitedly taking photos after the
show. "You are naturals! Misty, you belong on the stage."

I loved the attention she showered on me that evening. With so many siblings, it wasn't often that Mommy had time for just me. My hard work at school was sometimes rewarded, though. She gave me gifts when I was chosen as hall monitor or brought home good grades.

As much as I enjoyed performing with my siblings onstage, dance wasn't the first form of movement that mesmerized me. Gymnastics was what pulled me in, and it was because of one gymnast in particular: Nadia Comaneci. I was seven years old when I first saw the TV movie about her life. In 1976, she'd become the first woman to receive a perfect 10 in gymnastics at the Olympics. She was fourteen years old when she took home three gold medals.

I recorded the movie so I could watch it over and over. When that wasn't enough, I started watching gymnastics competitions on TV, and then I began to teach myself the moves. We were living with Robert and I had plenty of space to practice, with the large, grassy lawns in the front and back of the house. I learned the moves quickly, becoming my own teacher. My body bent with ease into back walkovers, cartwheels, and splits. I would pretend to be Nadia after I finished my routines, raising my arms with pride for my imaginary crowd. I always preferred the floor routines to the other gymnastics events, and soon I would realize the movement transfixed me because it was so close to dance.

Gymnastics was the only sport I enjoyed watching, but my family loved it all. Basketball, football, baseball—it didn't matter. Everyone except me would gather to watch whatever game was on, and everyone had a favorite team. The love for sports ran in our blood. Mommy was such a fan that before we were born, she was a Kansas City Chiefs cheerleader just so she could watch the games for free.

But when everyone else was crowded around the TV, I preferred to be in my bedroom, listening to my favorite songs and creating my own entertainment. At the time, I didn't know how to do much more than twist my hips from side to side and nod my head to the beat. I'd imitate the moves I saw in music videos and act out the lyrics, word for word. I was creating my own dance routines. I was choreographing.

Dancing was my escape. The movement and music combined made me forget about all the things that worried me. Like how we never had any money. Or Mommy's constantly changing boyfriends and husbands. And our cramped, uncomfortable living conditions.

In sixth grade, I signed up for another talent show. This time at Point Fermin Elementary with my two best friends, Danielle and Reina. I choreographed our routine, and even though they didn't share my passion for dance, I loved being back onstage, lip-synching and moving to the rhythm of the Mariah Carey song I'd chosen.

Normally, I was shy at school. I was anxious when I had to speak up or read in front of the class. I was so terrified of being late that I'd get to school an hour early. I didn't want to be called out for doing the wrong thing or being in the wrong place. But when it came to performing, I felt completely at home. All my anxieties faded and I felt strong. In control.

That confidence and passion for the spotlight is what convinced me to try out for the drill team when I got to Dana Middle School the next year. My big sister, Erica, had been a member of the team, and it was well-known for winning state competitions. I knew I wouldn't be satisfied with just a place on the team, though. I had my sights set on the top spot: captain.

I worked tirelessly on my choreography. One routine would be performed by every girl trying out for the team. The other was the one I'd use to audition for captain. I was nervous when I showed up for tryouts. But when it was time for my solo, I launched right into my routine, giving my best for the judges. The drill squad members who helped decide our fate didn't offer up any friendly reassurance. But the new coach, Elizabeth Cantine, smiled after I finished my routine.

I wouldn't find out whether I'd made the cut until later that evening. My stomach was in knots when the phone finally rang. It was the call I was hoping for. I'd made the drill team! Even better, I would be its new captain.

The team was big, made up of thirty girls. I was the youngest, and I didn't have much in common with the other members. I was in student government and still played with Barbies, while they were more interested in boys and makeup. But they respected that I was the one with CAPTAIN MISTY embroidered on the uniform we wore on game days. They knew I'd earned my spot because I was the best dancer. My shyness and anxiety disappeared when I was leading the team, calling out commands with authority.

Aten-hut! Left face!

The new coach, Elizabeth, had classical ballet training, and she wove some of that technique into our routines. She taught us basic steps, like the different types of turns. For *chaînés*, I spun across the room on the tips of my toes in a straight line, opening and closing my arms as I turned. And there were *piqué* turns, in which I stepped onto one foot and whipped around, bringing my other leg up to my knee. I'd never heard the French names of the steps Elizabeth taught us, but like the gymnastics I'd learned by myself years ago, the movement came naturally to me.

I used the new steps to help choreograph a routine, one I made up to Mariah Carey's "All I Want for Christmas Is You." I also created the costumes, pairing the new red leotards Elizabeth bought using money from the drill team's budget with skirts trimmed in fake fur that I'd sewed on myself. I knew the most important part was practice, and I worked my team hard. We even rehearsed on the weekends to make sure everyone knew the steps perfectly.

All the practice paid off—our Christmas performance got a standing ovation.

chapter 4

AFTER THE CHRISTMAS BREAK, ELIZABETH approached me.

"You know, you have the perfect physique for ballet and a natural ability," she said. "I know you go to the Boys and Girls Club after school. A friend of mine teaches a ballet class there. Her name is Cindy Bradley. Why don't you check it out?"

It was true that I went to the San Pedro Boys & Girls Club every day after school. It was two blocks from our school, and my siblings and I spent time there in the afternoons until Mommy picked us up after work.

But I didn't have any interest in ballet. I'd never seen a performance. And the thought of learning something new from a woman I didn't know made me nervous.

Not obeying Elizabeth's request would have made me more anxious, though, so I did as she asked. The ballet class was held in the gym of the Boys & Girls Club. I sat silently in the bleachers that afternoon, simply watching. The students were almost all girls, but there were a couple of boys, too. Most of them were younger than me.

After I'd been watching for about a week, Cindy, the teacher, came over to the bleachers.

"I see you sitting here every day," she said. "What are you doing?"

I explained that my drill team coach had sent me.

"She told me about you," Cindy said. "Why don't you come join me?"

I still felt too shy. The students on the gym floor looked as if they'd been taking lessons for a long time. Plus, they were decked out in proper dance gear: leotards, pretty pink tights, and ballet slippers. I didn't have any of those things.

"Don't worry about that," Cindy assured me. "You can just wear your gym clothes."

Sitting up in the bleachers, I couldn't stop thinking about everything that could go wrong. Like that I wouldn't be able to learn the steps. Or that I'd disappoint

Cindy, who would then have to tell Elizabeth how I'd failed. I could hear the whole conversation in my head.

"She couldn't follow a single thing I said," Cindy would say. *"This girl needs to stick to the drill team."*

It was another week before I worked up the courage to take class with the other students. I still didn't have a leotard or the right shoes. I wore a white T-shirt, long cotton shorts, and a pair of gym socks that would allow me to glide across the floor.

Embarrassed, I walked out to the middle of the gym to join the other dancers. I drew myself up to my full height and focused my eyes straight ahead. Then, for the first time in my life, I placed my hand on the long horizontal rail they used for support. The barre.

I didn't like it.

Where drill team was overflowing with energy, the hour I spent in the gym at the Boys & Girls Club was repetitive. Ballet seemed to be nothing more than learning where to place our feet and how to bend our arms. It didn't seem like dance at all.

I kept going to the Boys & Girls Club, as usual, but I didn't go back to ballet. For the next week, I avoided the gym, participating in other activities.

But Cindy didn't let me give up so easily. She found me about a week after I'd taken my first class and called me into the gym. She pulled me to the front of the room and my nerves took over. Once again, I was afraid of looking foolish. I didn't know as much as everyone else in the class, and I didn't like feeling so behind.

Cindy didn't make me do anything by myself, though. She used me to demonstrate moves to the rest of the class. As I stood in front, Cindy stretched my limbs into various poses. Under her direction, my feet, arms, and legs moved perfectly into positions that had official ballet terms. She told me I was one of a kind. That she'd never had a student like me.

I thought she was just saying that to make me feel better. But I suppose a part of me wanted to see if there was any truth to it. I slipped over to the barre with the rest of the students and officially rejoined her class.

Cindy taught us basic steps, the foundation of ballet. I started by learning the five positions.

First position: We stood with our heels touching and our toes pointed outward.
Second position: This was the same as first

position, but with several inches of space
between our feet.

Third position: We stood with one foot placed
in front of the other, with the heel of the front
foot touching the arch of the other.

Fourth position: Our feet were spaced about
twelve inches apart, with one foot turned out
in front of the other.

Fifth position: Our feet formed two parallel
lines, like an equal sign, with our legs turned
out and crossed one in front of the other.

I remember first executing the steps I'd eventually rehearse
and perform hundreds of thousands of times in my life. Like
when I twirled in place on one leg for the first time, executing
my first *pirouette*. My arms were strong but graceful, held in
a semicircle before me as I lifted my leg and turned my body
completely around. Or when I leaped high, one leg extended
straight in front and the other stretched behind me. It felt like
my body was doing the splits in the air, with my arms raised
up to the ceiling. I learned this was a *grand jeté*.

"It's just amazing that you can already do these things,"
Cindy said as she molded me into different positions.

It was as if I'd learned the movements in a past life and it all came back to me when I was in Cindy's class. Still, I worked hard to make sure I did my best at ballet, the same as I pushed myself in school and at drill team. The natural ability I had for dance didn't make me any less nervous about my place in the class. I didn't feel like I totally fit in.

For one, I still didn't have a leotard and tights, instead wearing my loose-fitting gym clothes. And second, I was much older than my fellow dancers. I was starting out at thirteen. Most dancers begin ballet lessons when they're as young as three or four. They had many more years of training than me. I became discouraged, wondering if I'd ever be able to reach their level.

But no matter how much I doubted myself, Cindy always believed in me.

chapter 5

CINDY'S JOB AT THE BOYS & GIRLS CLUB
wasn't permanent; she owned the San Pedro Dance Center.
Her studio was in the same community, but it was located
in an area where people had more money.

Cindy believed that everyone should be able to learn the
beauty and joy of ballet, even if they couldn't pay for lessons.
So she started a program with Mike Lansing, the director of
the San Pedro Boys & Girls Club, that would help bring the
most talented kids from my neighborhood into her studio.

"You need more intense training and the chance to be
with strong dancers who can push you," she said. It was
clear by then that I'd mastered the basics. "You'll get that
at my school, and we should start as soon as possible."

But ballet wasn't my dream at that point. I liked it, but I *loved* drill team. Not only that, but it felt more natural, like something I was supposed to do. My big sister, Erica, had been on the team, and Mommy had been a cheerleader for the Kansas City Chiefs.

When she couldn't convince me on her own, Cindy tried to talk to my mother. She sent notes home with me, addressed to Mommy. They said how much she wanted to continue my lessons at the San Pedro Dance Center. But the notes never made it home with me. I tossed them in the cafeteria trash cans or hid them in my folder, behind my homework.

Cindy wouldn't let it go. She saw so much promise in me that she offered to pay for the lessons I'd be taking, along with the leotard, tights, and shoes I'd need. She would also give me a ride to the studio after school each day. Cindy would take care of every barrier and excuse that could possibly stand in my way. I knew I had to tell Mommy.

I gave Cindy our number. I was so anxious about the idea of starting lessons at a real dance studio that part of me hoped Mommy would say no to her offer. I wasn't so lucky. Mommy thought it would be a great opportunity.

"You know, when you were a little girl, you loved ballet," she said.

I was shocked. I couldn't remember taking lessons anywhere besides the Boys & Girls Club. Mommy said she'd bought me a tutu for Halloween when I was four or five. She said I loved it so much I'd even slept in it!

"Miss Bradley seems to think you've got some potential," my mother said. "Let's give it a try and see how it goes."

Cindy's studio had gray walls and something called a sprung floor—a special floor that was easier on our joints than dancing on wood. There was no piano in the corner. Instead, she used a stereo for our background music. Most of the students at the San Pedro Dance Center were white, but I wasn't the only child of color. A lot of people think that ballet dancers should all look the same: thin and delicate, with white skin. Cindy thought different shapes, colors, and sizes should be represented to reflect the variety of talent in the ballet world. I feel lucky to have been nurtured by someone so supportive of my differences so early in my career.

There was Catalina, a Latina who is still one of my best friends today. I was so tiny for my age that she thought I was younger than her. She was ten and I was thirteen! One of my other good friends at the studio was an African American boy named Jason Haley. We understood each other. We were both members of the Boys & Girls Club, and like me, his home life was disruptive. He'd been moving back and forth between the houses of relatives since he was young. He was tall and graceful, but his natural talent didn't guarantee he'd arrive to class on time or show up to our performances. Our teachers didn't like that so much!

Cindy had such faith in me that she never treated me like a beginner. I took classes with the advanced levels, where I was dancing next to students who'd been studying ballet for years. The moves came easily to me. Cindy said I picked up ballet much faster than most students. She believed my technique was so strong that she trusted me to go *en pointe* only eight weeks after I'd been taking lessons at her studio.

I didn't realize how rare it was for me to go *en pointe* so early. It takes most young dancers years to master the technique of dancing on the tips of their toes. They have to practice and practice before their feet are strong enough to execute more challenging steps, like *pirouettes* and *fouettés* and *renversés*. She even caught that special moment on camera, documenting the first time I lifted myself up *en pointe*.

"The perfect ballerina has a small head, sloping shoulders, long legs, big feet, and a narrow rib cage," Cindy said.

That was the description of the ideal body for ballet according to George Balanchine, an influential choreographer who helped found the New York City Ballet.

"That's you. You're perfect," Cindy said. "You're going to dance in front of kings and queens. You will have a life most people cannot even imagine."

I wanted to believe Cindy because by then my relationship with ballet had changed. I was no longer reluctant to take lessons and I didn't worry that everyone else was so ahead of me. I loved ballet. I felt like I needed it. I wanted to excel at it.

But ballet was also important because it provided structure in my otherwise chaotic life. We were living in the motel, and it was getting harder to find a way to and from class at the studio. Most days Cindy would give me a ride after school, but sometimes I had to rely on Erica and her boyfriend, Jeff, to drive me across town. Jeff didn't always have time to drive us, so on those days, Erica would take the bus to the studio with me. The trip to the San Pedro Dance Center took an hour each way, and lots of nights we wouldn't arrive back at the motel until after dark.

Mommy didn't like all the time I was devoting to ballet—all the hours I spent each week dancing, not to mention the time it took to get to the studio and back. She was worried I didn't have enough time for my family and friends and wanted me to stop. "I know you're liking this class, but you'll only be a kid once," she said.

I told Cindy what Mommy had said the next day. She looked sick when the words sank in. There were tears in her eyes at the news that I'd have to quit dancing. She didn't argue. She just offered to drive me home.

I'd never told Cindy where I was living. She couldn't hide the shock on her face when she pulled up to the shabby motel I called home. Embarrassed, I thanked her for the ride and ran up the stairs of the building.

She followed me up to our room. And when Mommy opened the door, there was no more hiding. Cindy could see the blankets we used for makeshift beds on the floor each night, since my siblings and I slept in the living room.

Cindy and my mother talked for a long time that evening. They both cried as Mommy explained that with five other kids, she couldn't give me the attention I needed to keep up with my dance training. I think Cindy realized I might never return to ballet if she didn't step in and do something.

"I can't leave her," she said. "I want Misty to come live with me."

Mommy sighed. She must have known deep down that I would be better off staying with Cindy, who lived in a house with more space and fewer people. She could focus on raising not just a young girl, but a ballerina.

Mommy said yes. I could go.

chapter 6

EVERYTHING I NEEDED TO BRING WITH ME
fit into a backpack. Clothes were all I needed, really. Cindy
would provide everything else.

I'd be staying with her; her husband, Patrick; and their
three-year-old son. His name was Wolf but everyone called
him Wolfie. They lived in a condo two blocks from Cabrillo
Beach, by the Angel's Gate Lighthouse. Their home was
decorated with beautiful paintings and sculptures, and I'd
soon learn that it often smelled sweet, like cinnamon and
sugar, because Patrick liked to bake.

I didn't know this at the time, but Patrick didn't realize
Cindy was bringing me home with her. "Misty is here with
me," she told him. "She's going to be living with us."

She asked him to set another place at the table, and he never once showed surprise that I was not only a last-minute dinner guest but that I'd be staying with them for a while. We ate Chinese food that evening. When it was time to go to sleep, Cindy tucked me into the top bunk of the bed I'd be sharing with Wolfie. She kissed me good night and told me how happy she was that I was there with them.

My new situation was more common than some people might think. Often, gifted young athletes and dancers move in with their coaches or instructors to devote more time to improving their craft. I was following in Cindy's footsteps. Like me, she'd moved out of her own home when she was a teenager to focus on dance.

This was the first time I could remember the move to a new home not being filled with tension. Before, we were leaving behind stepfathers and boyfriends. Sometimes they were homes we loved and sometimes they were situations we feared. We never knew how our lives would be affected when we transitioned to a new home and life. I thought I'd be nervous staying in yet another new place, but the Bradleys were kind and always made me feel like I was welcome in their home.

★　★　★

A new location meant a new routine. When I lived with Mommy, I took the bus to school and sometimes I hopped back on it to go home too. Now Cindy dropped me off, and in the afternoons she picked me up to take me to the San Pedro Dance Center.

At school, I still led the drill team in our performances and daily practice, but my heart wasn't in it. The movement was so different from the powerful elegance of ballet. Drill team seemed too simple now. Unimaginative.

The drill team coach, Elizabeth Cantine, was supportive. She was friends with Cindy, and together they worked to give me the ballet education they believed I deserved. While my lessons were paid for by Cindy's scholarship, Elizabeth and her husband, Richard, bought all of my tights, leotards, and shoes. Pointe shoes are expensive, and ballet dancers wear them out quickly.

Elizabeth was supportive emotionally, too. She came to the studio to watch my classes, and she attended every one of my performances. Her home became so comfortable that many nights, I would sleep over. After a while, I considered Elizabeth my mentor and, eventually, she and Richard became my honorary godparents.

As I progressed in my ballet training, I learned that

perfecting basic technique is the key to performing more difficult steps. The classes we spent mastering *pliés*, when we bent our knees over our toes, slow and controlled, and *passé*, when we lifted the foot of our working leg above and behind the knee of our standing leg, would help prepare me for the quick footwork of *fouetté* turns. I couldn't wait to learn them, and Cindy showed me how to apply the basic steps.

"Now you *plié*," she'd say, guiding me. "Now swing your leg to the side. Then bring it into *passé*."

Once we'd begun to master the more advanced steps on our own, we learned how to dance with a partner: a *pas de deux*. Our usual teacher for partnering was a man named Charles Maple, though sometimes Cindy's husband, Patrick, led the class. Charles used to be a soloist with the American Ballet Theatre, one of the best ballet companies in the world.

He liked partnering with me to demonstrate during class. I could execute almost any move just by watching. I was a fast learner, and I had the skill to back it up. Charles, Cindy, and Patrick all marveled at my training. I didn't know they considered me so special that they would start to use a word to describe me. I was picking up on the material so quickly and performing the moves so well that they called me a "prodigy," a word I would hear many more times over the years.

chapter 7

LIVING WITH CINDY EXPOSED ME TO MORE
than just physical ballet training.

I'd never seen a professional dance performance, unless
you counted music videos. But when I lived with the
Bradleys, the football that my family had always watched
was replaced by recorded performances of the American
Ballet Theatre.

Founded in 1940, ABT is based in New York and
has earned the title of one of the greatest classical ballet
companies in not just the country, but the world. Some
of the most famous and talented ballet dancers have performed with ABT: Gelsey Kirkland, Mikhail Baryshnikov,
Natalia Makarova, Rudolf Nureyev, Paloma Herrera.

I became enthralled with these performances, but my favorite was the *pas de deux* from the ballet *Don Quixote*. The dance featured Mikhail Baryshnikov, who eventually went on to become ABT's artistic director, and Gelsey Kirkland, who had greatly inspired legendary choreographer George Balanchine. From the moment I saw that *pas de deux*, I wanted to be the character of Kitri. Her rebellious, feisty nature was conveyed in each move of the quick choreography, and I fell in love.

Gelsey Kirkland's version was my introduction to Kitri, but after I saw Paloma Herrera dance the role, she would become one of my idols.

Paloma was born in Buenos Aires and, like me, she was known as a prodigy. By the age of fifteen, she had already joined ABT's corps de ballet, the dancers who support the soloists and principal dancers. At nineteen, she was promoted to principal, the top spot in the company. I first saw Paloma dance live when Cindy took me to see *Don Quixote*; she played Kitri at the Dorothy Chandler Pavilion in Los Angeles.

The performance captivated me. And from that night on, I was determined to not only follow Paloma's career but try my hardest to model my own after hers.

I enjoyed living with the Bradleys. I was immersed in ballet training and culture, and they always treated me like a member of their family. We even had professional pictures taken of the four of us: Cindy, Patrick, Wolfie, and me. They displayed them proudly around our home.

I also grew close to Cindy's parents. Their names were Catherine and Irving, but I knew them as Bubby and Papa. They were so welcoming that Wolfie and I both had our own bedrooms at their house. Bubby and Papa also liked to share their faith with me. They were Jewish and sometimes I went to temple with them. We had Shabbat dinner each Friday to celebrate the day of rest. I learned the prayers, which were recited in Hebrew, and soon they were so familiar to me that I could say them by memory.

But as much as Bubby wanted to include me in her life, she didn't want me to forget about my background. One day she put on an old movie called *To Sir, with Love*. An actor named Sidney Poitier was the star of the film. She turned to me when it was over.

"He was the first black man to win an Oscar," Bubby explained. "He broke barriers, just like you."

Bubby didn't talk about my blackness often, but what

she had to say was always positive. At home, Cindy continued to make me feel special too.

"You're going to be a star," she said when we were sitting around the dinner table. "You're God's child."

She encouraged me not to straighten my hair. She liked it better in its natural state. Cindy believed that my brown skin and curly hair, the things that made me different in the ballet world and my new home, were beautiful.

Cindy made other big changes in my life too.

A few months before I turned fifteen, she enrolled me in an independent study program. We'd agreed I should switch to homeschooling so I'd have more time to train at the studio. I picked up my assignments and turned in the completed homework twice a month. I was able to spend as much time as possible dancing.

Cindy was a free spirit. She would rather make decisions with her heart than follow the rules. But when it came to my future, she was focused.

"You're going to be socializing with very important people," she said. She told me I needed to know how to behave in formal situations.

I learned how to set a proper table and that there are different forks for salad and cake. But Cindy wasn't just concerned with etiquette. She wanted me to take care of myself on the inside, too. Gone were the days of eating junk food for lunch and dinner. When I lived with Mommy, she didn't always have money for more than what we could buy in the motel vending machines. One of my favorite meals back then was spicy Cheetos corn chips, which I smothered with processed cheese and hot sauce.

At the Bradleys' house, I regularly ate fresh vegetables. I also began to eat food my mother didn't have the budget for, like shrimp. When I went back to the motel on weekends to see my family, I noticed right away that the meals weren't what I'd become used to. Mommy cooked with vegetables that she dumped out of a can, and now I could tell the difference. Suddenly I didn't have a taste for the food I had grown up eating.

Mommy didn't like that. She also didn't like that I had stopped straightening my hair and that I was wearing the beautiful, trendy clothes Cindy liked to buy for me.

"You're not a doll for her to dress up," Mommy complained, frowning. "And you're not her daughter. I can take you shopping." But I knew she didn't have the money to spend on clothes that Cindy did.

My mother became even more upset when performing

started to take up more of my time. Cindy booked me and the other kids from the studio for performances around town, including at the Special Olympics and the Taste of San Pedro. Once, I even danced by myself, *en pointe*, for the Los Angeles Dodgers.

I was so busy that I couldn't come home every weekend. Mommy started calling Cindy to complain. She wanted me to have a good life, but she was afraid Cindy was taking me away from her and my siblings.

I think she felt like the Bradleys were trying to become my new family.

chapter 8

MOMMY COULDN'T DENY THAT MY NEW LIFE brought me better opportunities.

Cindy had me performing all the time, and she was mindful about involving me in the black dance community. Once, I performed at a charity event that featured the great actress Angela Bassett. I was so nervous during the dress rehearsal when I got the chance to meet her. By the time I was fourteen, people were starting to notice me. Newspapers wrote articles about me. Everyone seemed to be fascinated that I had accomplished so much and that I'd started ballet so late in my life. On top of that, I was black, and you didn't see many brown-skinned dancers in the world of ballet.

Debbie Allen, a well-known actress and choreographer,

contacted Cindy around that time to see if I wanted to be a part of her production called *The Chocolate Nutcracker*. I'd danced the lead of Clara in a performance of *The Nutcracker* at San Pedro High School the first year I was training at Cindy's studio. *The Chocolate Nutcracker* was a version of the classic Christmas story that incorporated African dance. I was going to play the lead, Clare.

I worked hard, rehearsing for the performance. I practiced with private choreographers and learned different types of dance, including Brazilian and African. I danced *en pointe*, surrounded by other black dancers and live, banging drummers that kept the beat.

The performance was held at UCLA's Royce Hall and it was a success. I received a standing ovation! No matter how nervous I was about fitting in and meeting new people in the dance world, I felt right at home onstage. Completely comfortable in my own skin. Mommy was so proud of me. She cheered me on from the front row.

The news articles continued after that night. Debbie Allen talked about me in an interview with the *Los Angeles Times Magazine*. She described me as "a child who dances in her soul" and said she couldn't imagine me doing anything else.

I decided to quit the drill team about a year after I'd begun dancing. That way I would have time to focus even more on ballet. And soon after I'd danced the part of Clare in *The Chocolate Nutcracker*, I would get the chance to play my favorite role at the San Pedro Dance Center: Kitri in *Don Quixote*.

Cindy said the next step was to start entering competitions. I was gaining local attention, but she thought it was time for me to start attracting even more interest. The first competition she wanted me to enter was a big contest called the Los Angeles Music Center's Spotlight Awards. In addition to ballet, teenage contestants could compete in a number of categories, such as classical and jazz music, singing, and acting.

Winning a Spotlight Award would provide me with scholarship money, but it would also earn me respect in the ballet community. Previous winners have performed at prestigious places like the Alvin Ailey American Dance Theater, the Metropolitan Opera, and American Ballet Theatre.

Cindy and I decided I would audition with a piece from *Don Quixote*. I threw myself into practice. I knew I had to be as close to perfect as possible, so I took only one day off a week from rehearsing. My buildup to the competition was all captured on film. A local TV station was following a group of teens competing in the Spotlight Awards to feature on a program called *Beating the Odds*. I was one of those teens.

A few days before the awards, I began to have trouble executing my routine. The steps I'd be performing were complicated; the sequence included thirty-two *fouetté* turns. That would be challenging for a more experienced dancer, and I had been taking ballet for only two years.

I was anxious that I wouldn't be able to complete the *fouettés* during the competition. Cindy started to worry too, on the morning of the performance.

"You have to get this," she said. "This is your big chance. Gerald Arpino will be there."

Gerald Arpino had founded the Joffrey Ballet, a highly respected dance company based in Chicago. He was also the artistic director of the Joffrey, and would be a judge at the Spotlight Awards that year.

Just before the competition began, Cindy choreographed a new version of the sequence for me. It would feature only sixteen turns instead of thirty-two, so I wouldn't get over-whelmed when I was onstage. I wore a red tutu trimmed in gold, and even though I couldn't see them in the darkened theater, I knew Mommy, Lindsey, Cindy, and Bubby were all there, watching me.

I performed the new piece, my backup plan, and my execution was perfect. I was beaming when I finished, pleased and proud of my performance. I don't remember much after that, except that I won first place in the ballet category. My prize was $5,000.

Gerald Arpino found me backstage and immediately scooped me up in his arms. "You're my baby, you're my baby," he exclaimed. "You have to come dance with me! You have to come to the Joffrey!" That moment was captured by dozens of cameras and by KCET, the television station that was filming me for *Beating the Odds*. The image appeared in newspapers and on the front of a local TV guide.

Winning the competition, and Gerald Arpino's interest in me, meant that I was on my way up in the ballet world.

Now that I'd made a name for myself with the Spotlight Awards, Cindy wanted me to audition for summer programs.

Each year, the top ballet companies welcome young dancers into their studios for summer intensive programs. These sessions are a way for dancers to experience training in a professional environment. The companies are also looking closely at each person they admit into the program, in hopes that they will find future members.

I auditioned for the Joffrey and ABT. They had both offered me spots after I won the competition, but they needed to figure out how much scholarship money to award me. My other auditions were at the Dance Theatre of Harlem, the Pacific Northwest Ballet, the New York City Ballet, and the San Francisco Ballet.

Although there will never be total agreement over which company is the best, ABT is at the top of the list. At home, it's known as America's National Company. Its classically trained talent is matched by international companies such as the Paris Opera Ballet, the Royal Ballet in London, and the Bolshoi Ballet and Kirov Ballet (which is formally called the Mariinsky Ballet) in Russia.

Every company offered me a spot in their summer program, along with a scholarship, except for the New York City Ballet. I didn't understand why it was the only company that didn't want me, but Cindy had an idea. She thought it was because I was black.

I kept the rejection letter, but I didn't have time to dwell on it. I had to choose among the other programs, all of which had asked me to attend. San Francisco Ballet would pay for everything: my program tuition, room and board, and the plane tickets to get there and back. It was a great offer—too good to refuse. And it would be closer to my home in Southern California than any of the other programs that had accepted me.

I made my decision. I was going to study with the San Francisco Ballet.

chapter 9

MY TRIP TO SAN FRANCISCO WAS ONLY THE second time I'd flown on a plane. Despite how many times I'd moved and been thrust into new situations, I was nervous about the trip. Before, I always had Mommy and my siblings with me, or I was heading into a situation with someone I trusted, like when I moved in with the Bradleys. In San Francisco, I wouldn't know anyone.

All summer intensive students stayed at the University of San Francisco dorms. When I arrived at my room, I was greeted by a sign on the door:

I'M KAYAKO. KINDA QUIET AND SHY UNTIL I GET TO KNOW YOU.

I had a feeling Kayako and I would get along well.

I was right. Kayako was biracial, like me, only she was half black and half Japanese. I rarely saw other black ballet dancers. I wondered if we'd been placed together on purpose or by accident. It didn't matter, though. We were fast friends. Once we met Jessica, who was Asian American, we became a nearly inseparable trio.

We spent almost all of our time outside of class together. We went to amusement parks, movies, and the arcades on Pier 39. But during the day, I was on my own. I was one of the students with the least amount of experience, but the school's associate director, Lola de Ávila, decided I should be in the advanced classes. I had the perfect body for ballet, with my long neck, large feet, and long, thin legs that tilted backward. And it was as if I'd been performing the strong, graceful movements my whole life instead of only a couple of years.

But I still had a lot to learn. I was in classes with students from all over the country and around the world— Spain, Russia, Japan—and they'd all been studying ballet since they were little girls. I was so tired at the end of each day. My body wasn't used to such intense training. I was dancing *en pointe* for hours, until classes ended in the late afternoon. When I got back to the dorm, Kayako, Jessica, and I would soak our swollen feet in trash cans filled with ice water.

Lola de Ávila took me under her wing. She had trained in Spain, performed famous ballets such as *Giselle* and *Raymonda*, and had taught at the National Ballet of Spain. She praised me for how far I'd come with so little training, and she never made me feel bad for what I didn't already know.

I was lost when the class did *petit allegro*, a series of small, quick jumps. Normally I could pick up moves right away, even if I'd never learned the individual steps. But this time I had to move back from the class and watch, unable to keep up. Lola noticed and pulled me to the front, demonstrating each step of *petit allegro*. I used to be embarrassed when I was singled out in front of the other students, but now I knew that learning the correct technique was more important than my shyness.

In my *pas de deux* class, the teacher used me as a model to show the moves to the rest of the students, similar to Charles Maple back at Cindy's studio. "You see," he would say to the class as he lifted me into the air with what seemed like little effort. "This is what a classical line looks like. Extend! Balance!"

I called Mommy and Cindy a few times a week, and my entire family came up to San Francisco for the Fourth of July. We spent the weekend sightseeing. At the end of their trip, we all went out to breakfast.

"You know, Misty, we all miss you," Mommy said over pancakes. "I think when the summer is over, we need to start thinking about you coming back home to live with me."

I didn't say anything. I simply nodded, even though that wasn't what I wanted.

Three weeks later, the summer program came to an end. Lola called me into her office on the final day. She was sitting next to Helgi Tómasson, the artistic director of the San Francisco Ballet.

"You know how impressed we are with you, Misty," Lola said. "We think you have the potential to be a great dancer, but you need consistent training to refine your technique. We would like you to come to our school and study with us for the full year."

Helgi, who was normally a silent observer, spoke to me for the first time that day. "If you keep working hard, I can see you one day being a part of our company."

I'd known they were interested in me. When I'd first accepted the offer to attend the program, Lola had called to tell us the details of the summer intensive. She didn't have to do that; most schools would simply send a letter. That, along with the generous package they'd given, had made me think they might offer me a spot at their school.

But not everyone was happy about the news. When I returned to the studio, I overheard some of the other girls talking. "Why'd they ask *her* to stay?" one of them said. "She doesn't have enough training. Anyone could see that."

The summer intensive hosted about two hundred students that year. I was one of three girls and two boys in the program who had been asked to study year-round with the San Francisco Ballet. I'd thought I was good enough, but now I wasn't so sure.

Do I really deserve this? I thought. *So many of these other girls are so much more experienced, so much stronger. Why me?*

Though I was proud to be offered a spot, I knew I wouldn't be going. Mommy wanted me back home. And Cindy had told me that even if I was accepted, she thought I needed to keep training back at the San Pedro Dance Center before I went away to ballet school. I knew the San Francisco Ballet was respected and accomplished, and I appreciated how warmly Lola had treated me since I'd arrived. But what I really wanted was to attend ABT. I'd been enamored with the company since watching videos at the Bradleys' house. I wanted to follow in the footsteps of Paloma Herrera, and dancing in ABT's summer program would bring me one step closer.

I'd had a good time in San Francisco and learned a lot. I was sad to say good-bye to Kayako, Jessica, and my other new friends.

Cindy picked me up when I flew into Los Angeles International Airport. I knew she and Mommy didn't agree on how I should be raised. My mother wanted me to come back home and live with her, worried that I was pulling away too much from our family. And Cindy had seen that I held my own with dancers who had much more ballet training than me. She was more focused on my career than ever before.

But I didn't know how quickly my life would change yet again. Or how ugly things would become.

chapter 10

BACK AT THE SAN PEDRO DANCE CENTER, I
was able to show Cindy and Patrick how much my technique had improved since I'd been away.

Cindy admired my *temps de cuisse*, a step Lola had
taught me. She and Patrick watched as I drew one foot in
front of the other and lifted myself into the air, jumping
with both feet before I flawlessly landed on one of them. I
did it for them again and again. I was happy to make them
proud. But I was starting to wonder if it was time to move
on from Cindy's studio and train somewhere that could
challenge me more.

Mommy was still worried that I was spending too much
time away from her and my siblings. "They're trying to take

you away from me!" she yelled. "I'm your mother! You have a family! You don't need them."

I tried my best to convince her that the Bradleys weren't trying to turn me against her. But she wouldn't listen. She'd made up her mind. When I was visiting her and my brothers and sisters at the motel one weekend, she said I'd have to move back home. She thought the training and offers from the San Francisco Ballet proved that I'd outgrown Cindy's instruction.

Mommy didn't want me to quit ballet. She just wanted me to live at home while I trained. Elizabeth Cantine, my old drill team coach, helped my mother find a new dance studio to continue my lessons. And there would be no more homeschooling; she arranged for me to enroll at my old high school.

I was devastated. I knew that maybe Cindy didn't have anything more to teach me herself. But all the training and opportunities I'd been given in ballet were because of Cindy's belief in me, her dedication to my future. I wondered how I would be able to continue dancing without her in my life.

The morning after Mommy called Cindy to let her know I would be moving back home, Cindy picked me up at the motel. She looked so sad when I got in the car. Seeing that look on her face frightened me. She asked me if I'd ever heard of the word "*emancipation*."

I knew the definition: freedom.

"A lot of performers become emancipated," Cindy explained. "It's something they seek to have independence from their parents, when they feel they can make better decisions than them about their careers and their lives."

I felt like my heart was going to beat out of my chest. It didn't stop when Cindy told me that instead of school, she was taking me to meet one of her friends.

We met him at a coffee shop on the other side of San Pedro, near Cindy's studio. Her friend was a lawyer named Steven Bartell. I was still a few years shy of eighteen, so I'd have to go to court if I wanted to become emancipated from Mommy. If the court approved my case, I'd be able to make the decisions that had been up to my mother. I would choose where I lived, where I took classes, where and how I went to school. I listened as Steven explained everything.

Then he asked what I wanted to do.

I wasn't sure.

I knew Mommy loved me, but my life with her hadn't

been easy. She was an adult—my mother—but I sometimes wondered if she should be in charge of my life. She wasn't always the most responsible mother, but it would break her heart if the court granted me emancipation.

Ballet was so important to me, though. Cindy had been telling me since we first met that ballet would take me places I couldn't imagine. And I believed her.

"Yes," I finally told Steven. "I want to be emancipated."

He and Cindy didn't want me to be there when they talked to Mommy, so I stayed with another student from the dance studio. I was too dazed to talk or eat or think straight. I couldn't stop worrying about what Cindy and Steven were telling my mother. I wondered what Mommy would think about my decision, and how my siblings would take the news.

Three days passed before I heard from Steven Bartell. He told me I needed to pack my things and come with him. Mommy had called the police and reported me missing. She'd also called local news stations and newspapers. She met us at the police station and hugged me tight against her as soon as she saw me.

I didn't try to hide that I was crying on the way back to the motel. I thought that leaving Cindy behind meant my ballet career was over. I thought I would no longer get to do the one thing I loved most in life.

I resented being back at the Sunset Inn.

Inside, it was too small to keep tidy. There were too many of us living in the tiny space. And outside, the building was dirty and loud. I was back to eating the food Cindy wouldn't allow at her house. I missed the clean, quiet condo I'd lived in with the Bradleys. I was mad at Mommy for making me come back home, and I'd hide out in the bathroom so I didn't have to talk to my family.

Even worse, my mother filed a restraining order against the Bradleys. That meant she wanted an order from the court that would not allow Cindy or Patrick to be near me. I wouldn't be able to see them anymore, or talk to them. Mommy hired a famous lawyer named Gloria Allred. After that, we were constantly followed by the news media. They shoved cameras in our faces at the courthouse, and some days they'd be waiting outside the front door of our motel.

Sometimes I looked at Cindy and Patrick when we were sitting in the courtroom. They were quiet, but they couldn't hide how upset they were. They were determined to get me back. They argued that I'd have a better life and career if I lived with them. Cindy even said to one reporter that she would have adopted me if I'd agreed to it.

The case went on, though, and eventually everyone became too tired to keep fighting for what they believed. Gloria, our lawyer, helped me withdraw my emancipation request. The court would not serve the Bradleys with a restraining order because they weren't doing anything wrong. They weren't threatening Mommy, me, or my brothers and sisters.

Finally, the court case was over. And I didn't know it at the time, but over the next ten years or so, I'd see Cindy and Patrick only a few times.

The drama wasn't over yet, though.

The court case had been covered by the media, including the *Los Angeles Times* and an entertainment show called *Extra*. Mommy started fielding calls from people who wanted to make movies about our situation. Cindy continued to give interviews to the press, and Mommy was angry about it. She said Cindy was making her look like a bad mother.

"We've got to make sure we get our side of the story out there," Mommy said, determined.

Soon after that, she would get the chance.

Producers from a talk show named *Leeza* called. They were interested in my story and wanted Mommy to talk about what had happened with Cindy. I didn't want to go, but my mother said I wouldn't have to sit with her onstage, in front of the cameras. I would stay in the audience with my brothers and sisters.

The taping would be the first time I'd seen Cindy since we were at the courthouse. Mommy picked me up from school in a black limousine, with all of my siblings squeezed inside. I was embarrassed. Although I'd grown comfortable being in the spotlight when I was leaping powerfully across the stage, I didn't like that sort of attention in my regular life. The limo was too loud and too big to be parked in front of San Pedro High.

Once we were at the show, I sat next to my sister Erica in the audience. Our mother was onstage, and Cindy was there, too, but she wouldn't be in the same room as us. We watched her interview on a monitor.

I was scared when Leeza Gibbons, the host, came into the audience to ask me questions. Mommy told me Leeza might want to hear from me, but I didn't like having to talk about what had happened in front of so many people. I started crying. And my big sister stepped in to save me.

"You tried to destroy our family," Erica yelled at Cindy's face on the screen. "We'll never forgive you for what you tried to do."

Finally, the show was over, and the limo took us home to the motel. The next day at school, my classmates said they'd seen me on TV. I was embarrassed that they'd watched the whole thing—Mommy and Cindy disagreeing over what was best for me, me breaking down into tears.

Everyone knew the details of my personal life now. And I didn't have Cindy. But even without her, I would still have dance.

And, at last, all the fighting between Mommy and the Bradleys was over too.

chapter 11

DESPITE THE MESS I'D BEEN DEALING WITH, I was back in classes at San Pedro High School. I was trying to pretend my life was normal. But it was hard to walk the halls every day when everyone knew what was going on at home.

I also went back to dancing, this time at a studio called the Lauridsen Ballet Centre. It was located in Torrance, a city several miles from San Pedro. The students were welcoming. They made no mention of me being on television or the fact that I was already so well-known. The studio and Diane, the owner and teacher, were new. But I felt comfortable being back in front of the barre and strengthening my technique with the other students *en pointe*.

I made friends quickly, with two girls in particular: Kaylen Ratto and Ashley Ellis. Like Jessica and Kayako at the summer intensive, I formed a tight bond with my new friends. In fact, we're still close today, so many years after I met them. I'm grateful that they were there for me. Their friendship was a bright spot during a dark time in my life.

Lauridsen wasn't a big studio, but the students and lessons were more advanced than what I'd been exposed to at the San Pedro Dance Center. Diane taught me how to improve my technique. Sometimes that meant I had to start over, relearning steps I'd first executed at Cindy's studio.

Diane was kind to me, but she was a tough instructor. She made sure I was dancing to my best ability and gave me gentle reminders in class. "Don't sit into your hyperextended knees," she would say, gently guiding my body into the proper posture. Cindy had always treated me like I was the best and the brightest in her class, even though the other students had been dancing much longer than me. In Diane's classes I didn't stand out among the rest of the girls. And blending in was exactly what I needed.

Life began to settle down in the weeks after I returned home.

Mommy got a new job, and we were finally able to move

out of the motel. She found a two-bedroom apartment in a peaceful part of San Pedro. We no longer had to walk through the grimy passageways of the building or listen to the noise from the highway. And I didn't have to sleep in the living room anymore. My younger sister, Lindsey, and I had our own bedroom.

This move felt different from all the others. We didn't bring along one of Mommy's boyfriends or move into one of their houses. We weren't running away from anyone. This apartment felt like a place just for Mommy and us. A place for our family.

With my home life more quiet now, I was able to think about the upcoming summer intensive auditions. Each company held classes for a few weeks that would serve as tryouts. They listed their schedules in the back of *Dance Magazine*, and we'd show up with fifty or sixty other students to try to win a spot in the program.

The audition was like the ballet classes most of us had taken hundreds of times. We started at the barre and then moved to the center. But our every move was being watched from the moment class started until the second it ended.

ABT invited me to audition. The program director,

Rebecca Wright, had seen me win the ballet prize at the Spotlight Awards. She was already familiar with my dancing. But I still had to try out with everyone else. Elizabeth Cantine and her husband took me to the audition and waited for me outside the room.

I heard from ABT two weeks later. I'd been accepted, and they offered me a full scholarship. My dream of attending ABT was going to come true!

In San Francisco, all the summer intensive attendees had lived in the dorms. In New York, I stayed in a nunnery, with the Carmelite Sisters Teresas of San Joseph. The convent, located in Greenwich Village, was different from what I was used to. But it was peaceful, safe, and within walking distance to the rehearsal studios.

The nuns were nurturing and made us breakfast and dinner each day. They spoke only Spanish, so I couldn't have conversations with them. They woke us every day at seven a.m. through the intercoms wired into each of our rooms.

Like last summer, I had a roommate. But this time I didn't share my room with girls from the same program. I had a few different roommates: my friends Margeaux,

Kaylen, and Ashley, who were all students with me at the Lauridsen Ballet Centre back in California. Margeaux and Kaylen were dancing in the Joffrey Ballet's summer intensive. Ashley was studying at ABT with me.

The very first day, two important people at ABT wanted to talk to me: John Meehan and Kirk Peterson. John had once danced as a principal with ABT. Now he was the artistic director for the Studio Company, where younger dancers gained professional experience before being promoted to the main company. Kirk had been a principal dancer in the San Francisco Ballet's company, as well as at ABT. He had taken on the position of resident choreographer and ballet master for ABT, and was also doing so for the summer program.

I sat down and waited to hear why they'd called me in.

"We've heard your story, Misty," Kirk said, "and we want to know more."

So I told them everything. How I'd started at the Boys & Girls Club and about my win at the Spotlight Awards. I talked about my favorite performances, when I'd danced as Kitri in *Don Quixote* and Clara in *The Nutcracker*. I confessed that I'd always wanted to dance with ABT.

After I finished talking, they said how gifted I was. They believed in my talent so much that John said I could expect an invitation to ABT's Studio Company soon.

I'd just arrived at ABT and it seemed like my dreams were becoming reality.

chapter 12

NEW YORK CITY WAS SO DIFFERENT FROM
San Pedro.

For one, it was constantly busy. People were always
walking, driving, and riding bicycles. The gritty streets
buzzed with the electricity of the city, and the air carried so
many different smells. Also, it was incredibly humid, not
like the dry heat I was used to in Southern California.

After feeling so on display for so long with the battle
between Cindy and my mother, I was happy to be in a place
that was always bustling. I thought no one would notice me
on the crowded island of Manhattan.

I was wrong.

"Hey," a man said, stopping me as I walked down the

street. "Aren't you that little girl everyone was fighting over in California?"

I'd felt like being in New York meant I was starting with a clean slate. Now I wondered if the drama of my past would follow me for the rest of my life.

At ABT, I also had to get used to my new practice space.

The company rehearsed at 890 Broadway, using five studios spread out on two floors. Each studio had a piano, equipment to watch videos of performances, and mirrors that covered two whole walls from top to bottom. There were two huge dressing rooms, a physical therapy room with exercise machines, and a massage room where a therapist would help relieve the pain in our sore limbs.

As summer intensive students, we weren't supposed to explore the empty rooms around the rickety old building. Besides, there wasn't much time to wander. We were usually dancing. And at lunchtime we were too exhausted and hungry to do anything but eat and rest our tired muscles before going back to class.

One day, though, I decided to walk around. I slipped through the quiet, musty corridors until I found myself in an empty studio. Or, I'd thought it was empty when I walked in. But standing in front of me was Paloma Herrera. *The* Paloma Herrera whose career I'd been following since I first saw her perform as Kitri in Los Angeles.

She was talking on the phone and stretching her leg. She wore her dark hair in a loose bun, and she wasn't as tall as I'd thought she'd be. She had been such an inspiration to me. It felt like Paloma Herrera was one of the main reasons I'd made it to ABT in the first place. So I couldn't walk away without saying something. Anything.

Finally, I gathered my courage and I said hello in a tiny voice.

She didn't say anything back to me.

I walked out of the studio.

I was disappointed. I admired her so much and she'd seemed so unfriendly. But I would later come to understand why she'd seemed cold. She had worked hard to get where she was. She had started in the company when she was very young. Like my brown skin, her age made her different in the ballet world. It meant she had to work harder to prove that she belonged.

That first meeting wasn't what I'd thought it would be. Yet one day Paloma and I would not only dance together but become very good friends.

★ ★ ★ ★

The summer intensive was fun but exhausting. We spent seven hours a day practicing our technique. Then we'd go home with swollen feet and tired muscles. But all of our hard work was leading up to the recital, which would be held at the end of the program.

I would dance two parts. One was a *pas de deux* that Kirk Peterson, the ballet master, had choreographed. My second role would be a piece from the ballet *Paquita*. Up to that point, I'd only performed classical ballet, except for the part of Clare in *The Chocolate Nutcracker*. I was able to easily move between the modern choreography of Kirk's piece to the classical style of *Paquita*.

My friend Ashley Ellis performed a solo that night, and we both managed to impress the other students. Our dancing was so similar that they called her "the white Misty." We had identical bodies and exceptional technique, and we both attended the Lauridsen Ballet Centre back in Torrance.

After the show, I was summoned to talk to Kevin McKenzie, ABT's artistic director, and John Meehan. "You were wonderful tonight, Misty," John said. And then he officially asked me to join ABT's Studio Company!

As much as I'd been expecting him to invite me, I was still in shock. My dreams were all coming true. But I didn't know what to do. I was still in high school. I was only sixteen years old. I told them I had to ask my mother.

Mommy thought I needed to finish high school. And she was concerned about how much of my time ballet had already taken up: living with Cindy, then going to San Francisco and now New York. She thought I needed to spend more time with our family.

But at the end of the call, she said, "It's up to you. I think the year will fly by, and hopefully they'll make you the same offer next summer. But it's your dream, and I want you to feel good with the final decision."

I wouldn't have to quit school if I accepted ABT's offer. I'd still be able to earn a high school diploma while I was dancing. In addition to a spot in the Studio Company, Kevin and John offered me enough money to pay for my ballet gear—leotards, tights, and pointe shoes—and travel. Again, it was an offer that seemed too good to pass up.

But I kept thinking of my family. Erica was pregnant and soon I would be an aunt to her little girl. And home in San Pedro was finally comfortable. Mommy and I were getting along better than ever in the apartment we shared with Lindsey.

I knew what I had to do. I met with Kevin and John to tell them my decision.

"I want to finish high school back home," I said. "I hope you still want me next year."

The smiles and understanding on their faces told me that wouldn't be a problem.

chapter 13

MOMMY WAS RIGHT—THE NEXT YEAR DID
fly by.

I attended my senior year at San Pedro High and still
took classes at the Lauridsen Ballet Centre. ABT had given
me a Coca-Cola Scholarship, which went toward the cost of
my lessons and pointe shoes. I heard from Kevin and John,
who promised me a spot would be waiting for me in the
Studio Company when I graduated. I went to my senior
prom and then, in June, I finished school and headed back
to New York City to dance.

I didn't go back to the convent that summer. I had
another place to stay, the home of Isabel Brown. Isabel
was famous in ballet circles. Her whole family was

famous—they were known as the Brown Dynasty. They had a rich history with ABT. Isabel had been a member of the company in the 1940s and 1950s, and that's where she met her husband, Kelly, a dancer. Two of their children also danced with ABT: Ethan was a soloist and Leslie became a principal dancer, like her mother.

It was a big deal to be invited to stay in Isabel's home. Her Upper West Side brownstone was filled with antiques, and the decorations were exquisite. The Browns were so well-known in the ballet world that a movie had been made about them. It was called *The Turning Point*; Shirley MacLaine played the role based on Isabel. Mikhail Baryshnikov also starred in the film, along with Leslie, Isabel's daughter.

My second summer at ABT ended up being a summer of firsts. It was the first time I worked with Twyla Tharp, a famous choreographer who'd collaborated with ABT for decades. My friend Ashley was back at ABT with me, and Twyla worked with us on our starring roles in the final performance of the program.

And at the end of the summer, Kevin McKenzie, the artistic director, said that he wanted me to apprentice with the main company before I became a member of the Studio

Company that fall. That meant traveling to China—my first international trip.

Everything was so new and fresh. I knew I had to write it all down in my journal so I wouldn't forget those feelings:

> *Kevin said congratulations on the performance and congratulations on having a contract. I was in shock. . . . He told me that I was special and they would keep an eye on me. He said that he couldn't believe how strong my contemporary work was and how I was so grounded within it, yet so uplifting and strong in classical. It was a great surprise.*

I was only seventeen, almost eighteen, when I traveled with the main company to China. Over those two weeks, we visited Shanghai, Taipei, and Singapore. I performed as part of the corps de ballet in *La Bayadère*, dancing as a flower girl and in a waltz routine. In our free time, we were happy to be tourists, going to the Bihai Jinsha Water Park and the Chenghuang Temple in Shanghai.

Being in China, dancing alongside principals and

soloists I'd admired for years, was an amazing experience. And I had something to look forward to when I got back to New York.

It was time for me to join ABT's Studio Company.

The Studio Company was like a practice run before we joined ABT's main company. There were twelve of us: six girls and six boys. I knew most of them from the summer program, so we became a close crew. We spent a lot of time training together and visited places like Cape Cod, Buffalo, and even Bermuda, where we performed at theaters and schools.

My best friend in the company—we thought of each other as soul mates—was Leyla Fayyaz. Like me, she had been an apprentice with ABT's main company in China. She also had a mixed-race background; Leyla was Cuban, Lebanese, and Persian. We wandered around New York City together, and I don't know how I would have gotten through my first year without her.

I was proud to dance the role of Aurora, the lead in *Sleeping Beauty*, during nearly every show with the Studio Company. I performed the *pas de deux* with two men who are in ABT with me today: David Hallberg, who is currently a principal, and Craig Salstein, who dances as a soloist. I loved being in the Studio Company and I felt welcome there, like I was starting to learn who I really was.

I felt like the few months I'd lived with Cindy, when I was confident and not afraid to be myself.

chapter 14

I JOINED THE CORPS DE BALLET AT ABT when I was nineteen.

My ultimate dream was to become a principal dancer. Those are the dancers who perform leading roles and become the stars of the company. The corps de ballet is a chorus of dancers that supports the soloists and principals, but it's important on its own too. Without the corps, there would be no dance of the little swans, the famous *pas de quatre*—dance with four people—in Tchaikovsky's *Swan Lake*. A ballet without a corps would be like a rock concert without backup singers and musicians—they are the backbone of the company and help create the beautiful environments and atmosphere as the story is being told.

I felt like I was starting over when I was promoted to the corps. All my life, people had known about me. People like Lola de Ávila and Cindy had called me a prodigy. They'd always been in my corner, wanting me to do my best so I could advance to the top. The main company at ABT wasn't like that. The dancers didn't care what I had done before or where I'd been. All that mattered was now. And I was the new kid on the block.

The Studio Company had been so comfortable that I'd felt like I was coming out of my shell. But once I joined the main company, I started to retreat again. It wasn't just the other dancers who intimidated me. Some of the teachers seemed as if they couldn't understand why I'd been promoted. I don't know how much of that was true and how much I'd imagined, but like when I'd first started dancing at the Boys & Girls Club, I felt like I didn't fit in.

The world of ballet didn't seem created for a girl like me. I didn't come from a rich family that had been paying for their children's ballet lessons since they could walk. I was a late bloomer, starting ballet when I was only thirteen. I'd grown up moving as often as my mother changed boyfriends, and we didn't always know where we'd get our next meal. I was lucky enough to have people who believed in me and had offered to pay for my expensive training and the shoes, leotards, and tights that I wore out so quickly.

But it wasn't just the differences in how we'd grown up. In ABT, I was "the only one." The only black dancer in the entire main company, which consisted of eighty dancers. I was used to this in some ways. I'd lived with the Bradleys, who were all white. I'd gone to Jewish services at the temple with Cindy's parents, and there were no brown-skinned people there. But while I'd noticed being the only one before, no one had ever made me feel bad about it. In fact, they'd always celebrated what made me different.

Unfortunately, that wouldn't always be true once I became a professional dancer.

Ballet companies are known for creating beautiful performances, but behind the scenes, they operate a lot like a machine.

Dancers usually go through certain steps to make it to the main company. They start out in the school as ballet students, training to become professionals. The most talented dancers advance to the Studio Company. There they continue training, but they also begin performing, learning what it's like to rehearse and dance as part of a unit. Most of these dancers are then promoted to the main company.

The corps de ballet is usually made up of about fifty dancers. The rest of the members are either soloists or principals—the cream of the crop. There are usually about twelve soloists and twenty principal dancers in the company.

At ABT, we dance during two different seasons. The fall season lasts for three weeks to a month. The performances take place at the Koch Theater at Lincoln Center in our home base of New York City. We dance for eight weeks during the spring season and perform at the Metropolitan Opera House. Sometimes we have a winter season; this is when we perform the famous *Nutcracker* for about four weeks, at the Brooklyn Academy of Music.

The company starts rehearsing in September. When we're not performing during our designated seasons, we tour around the country and overseas. We only get two months off per year, during the summer. We call those weeks "lay-offs." During that time, I'm free to dance in other projects. This helps me maintain my technique so I'm ready to start the new season when fall begins.

We train very hard during the year. When we're still working on the ballets for our seasonal shows, we dance for about nine hours a day. Our morning begins with a ballet class that lasts an hour and a half. We practice barre and center work so that we can keep up our strength and technique. Then we work on the ballets we'll be performing for seven hours, from noon to seven o'clock at night. Once we've started performing, we dance even longer: Our evenings end just before midnight.

I take ballet classes year-round, even when we're off in the summer. Our bodies are our instruments, and ballet is so demanding that it's essential for dancers to stay in shape. I also keep my body toned through other classes, like cardio and a series of exercises called Pilates. It's important to maintain our technique and physical fitness because that's how we're chosen for roles in the different ballets.

Sometimes choreographers choose a small group of dancers to help develop a piece. Being selected to work on new dances means that sometimes the choreographer will assign us a lead role in the performance. But we never hold auditions within the company. ABT's artistic director, Kevin McKenzie, will observe us in classes and performances. Then he decides who will dance the major parts. The process to determine who will be promoted to soloist or principal dancer is similar at ABT. We don't hold auditions, but we know our progress is always being watched.

I was working toward that promotion even as I danced in the corps de ballet. But I'd barely signed the contract to dance with the company for my first year when my dreams were abruptly put on hold.

Summertime had arrived, and I'd been dancing with other choreographers and companies who had seen me perform with ABT and wanted to work with me. I was rehearsing with a choreographer from another company. We were dancing a contemporary piece, which was different from the classical work I'd been rehearsing and performing with ABT all year.

I moved and suddenly a terrible pain shot through my lower back. I knew I shouldn't continue dancing without going to the doctor, but I did. For two weeks.

When I finally went in to get tests done, I found out I had a stress fracture in my lower back. Stress fractures are not uncommon in ballet. We have such steady, difficult rehearsals and performances that nearly every dancer will become injured at some point in his or her career. I'd been lucky to catch my stress fracture early. They usually build up over many months without showing signs that something's wrong.

Right around that time, Kevin called me in. ABT was preparing for the upcoming season, and he'd chosen me as the lead in *The Nutcracker*. He wanted me to dance the role of Clara. It felt like fate. I'd loved playing Clare in Debbie Allen's *The Chocolate Nutcracker*. The performance had made people notice me and had put me on the radar. It was when I first started hearing the word "prodigy." I couldn't bear the thought of turning down the role of Clara.

But ultimately, I had to say no. My back still wasn't better, and I couldn't dance the role the way I wanted. Or the way Kevin expected me to.

I spent the next six months in a back brace. I had to wear it twenty-three hours a day, including while I slept. The only time I could remove it was when I took a bath. The six months after that, I spent in physical therapy, trying to retrain my body to move freely without the brace.

It was disappointing. I had come so far, working my way up from the summer programs to the Studio Company. Now I'd finally been promoted to the main company, and I wouldn't get the chance to dance with everyone else. I had to sit out the whole year to make sure my back healed the way it was supposed to.

Back then I didn't know that before my injury was the

only time I'd be asked to play the role of Clara. I didn't know how much would change once I returned to ABT a year later. I knew they'd have to replace me for the performance, but I didn't understand what that would mean for my future.

This is just something I'm going through, I thought. *When I go back, I'll pick up right where I left off.*

chapter 15

I SPENT MY RECOVERY TIME BACK HOME IN
San Pedro.

Mommy spoiled me while I was there, and I spent a lot
of time with Elizabeth Cantine, my old drill team coach,
and her husband, Dick. In a way, I felt like the extra time
allowed me to go back and relive my high school years. I'd
been so immersed in ballet and so terrified of new situations back then that I'd missed out on a lot of things. Now
I could spend my free time going to bonfires on the beach
with my friend Catalina, whom I'd met at Cindy's school.
I learned how to drive. I went on a cruise with my friend
Leyla and her family; we traveled to the sun-soaked coun-
tries of Mexico and Jamaica.

I began to exercise again, training with Diane, my former ballet teacher, and taking Pilates classes. I needed to go back to ABT strong and in shape so I could show Kevin and the company that my injury wasn't going to stop me.

I returned to New York City rested and ready to dance as part of the corps. I'd been back a few times while my injury was healing. I saw a doctor for my regular physical, and he had some concerns. He was worried my bones weren't strong enough to support my intense rehearsal and performance schedule. He also thought my body wasn't growing like it should be. I was nineteen years old and didn't yet weigh one hundred pounds.

He put me on hormones to help me start growing. They worked. I gained ten pounds in a few weeks and began to develop curves. I wasn't used to the new weight, and my body looked so different when I caught a glimpse of myself in the mirror.

When people think of ballerinas, they usually imagine a certain type of look: a small and thin dancer with creamy white skin and golden locks. Because of my coppery skin, I'd never looked like most of the people I'd danced with. But now, with my new body, I looked even less like the dancers people expected to see onstage.

In reality, I have a body that's ideal for dance. My limbs are long and incredibly flexible. I have knees that bend backward even when my posture is tall, and I have a long neck like the graceful swans we imitate in *Swan Lake*. My muscles are strong, which allows me to rehearse and perform turns and leaps over and over again each day for months on end.

I'd been used to sticking out because of my skin color, but now there was something else different about me.

When I got back to ABT, we were getting ready to perform *Swan Lake* and *Giselle*. As a member of the corps, I regularly traded costumes with the other dancers. Probably one reason ballet companies like their dancers to all be the same size is because it's cheaper to share costumes instead of fitting each dancer for her own.

But suddenly I could no longer fit into the same costumes the other girls wore. They were too tight on me. They had to be tailored by the wardrobe staff to fit my body.

It wasn't long before I was called in by the company staff to talk about my weight. They didn't tell me to lose weight—not in those exact words. Because the truth is that even with my new body, I was still considered thin by normal standards. I was only five feet two and didn't weigh much more than one hundred pounds. Instead of telling me to "lose weight," they had a special word they used.

"You need to 'lengthen,' Misty," one of the staffers said. "Just a little, so that you don't lose your classical line."

Who do they think they're talking to? I thought. *I have so much talent. Why do I have to be stick thin?*

I thought that if I could dance perfectly in rehearsals and performances, no one would care that my physique had changed. They wouldn't be distracted by the curves that now enhanced the lines of my body.

But I knew that wasn't true. My body wouldn't fit in at ABT, and it wasn't right for the classical roles that were my favorite. And then, one day, my fears were confirmed by someone who had nothing to do with the ballet world at all.

I was with my friend Leyla and we'd just met a guy. I told him I was a ballerina. The words flowed easily from my lips like they did anytime someone asked about my life.

But he looked like he didn't believe me. "No way," he said. "There's no way you could be a ballerina and be as big as you are. Ballerinas are thin."

Eating disorders are often associated with ballet dancers. Everything we do is dependent on our bodies and we're expected to look a certain way. Some dancers do have trouble with the unspoken pressure and develop unhealthy eating habits. Anorexia, in particular, is the eating disorder most people connect to ballet. But I've been with ABT for sixteen years, and I can count the number of dancers I've known with anorexia on one hand.

I never thought of starving myself or making myself vomit to keep the weight off. But after the talk with the ABT staff and the guy who didn't think I could be a ballerina, I started to believe I was fat.

I worried about it constantly, sure that everyone around me was thinking of how big I was. All I wanted to eat were foods that had little nutritional value, like cake and hot dogs. But I was too afraid of what people would think if they saw me eating what I'd been craving.

I'm huge, I thought. *What's it going to look like for me to go up to the counter and order two hamburgers and fries?*

I decided to start eating the fattening foods in private. There was a Krispy Kreme near me that would deliver to my apartment. But I had to order at least two dozen doughnuts for them to deliver. So I would buy twenty-four doughnuts. And then I would binge: I would eat almost all of them at once.

I felt good at first, when I was eating. And as I took bite

after bite of the sugary, sticky doughnuts, I would think about what ABT had said. *Ha! They want me to lose weight,* I thought, feeling rebellious. *I'll eat what I want!*

I always regretted my binge the next day. I didn't like how bloated I looked in the mirrors that lined the dance studios. Even worse, I'd feel ashamed about how much I'd eaten. But not ashamed enough to stop.

I was still dancing for hours and hours each day, so binge-eating fattening foods didn't make me gain weight. But the company staff noticed I wasn't losing weight. I wasn't "lengthening." So we had more talks.

"We believe in you, Misty," they would say. "We want to push your talent, but your line is not as lean and classical as it was before. We'd like to see you get that back."

I didn't understand how my body worked at first. I put on muscle easily, which meant I had to adjust the way I did cardio exercises. I also changed my diet. I cut out things that make me gain weight, like doughnuts, potato chips, and foods that contain a lot of salt or flour and white sugar. I also cut out beef, chicken, and pork; the only meat I eat now is seafood.

I learned how to take care of my body so it would remain strong through my rehearsals and reliable during performances. I changed my diet and exercise routine to keep myself healthy and fit. But I didn't lose my curves and muscles. They are part of what makes me Misty Copeland, and I was still working just as hard as the Misty who didn't weigh even a hundred pounds when she joined ABT. I was still giving my all in performances, even if my body had changed.

The company staff noticed. They stopped calling me in to have meetings about my weight. They began to accept me for me.

chapter 16

I'VE ALWAYS WANTED TO STAND OUT IN the ballet world. I dreamed of performing on the biggest stages in the world, being celebrated for my dancing.

But the truth is that I've always stood out for one particular reason. Ballet is a world full of ivory-skinned dancers. People are surprised to see a brown woman dancing alongside them.

In *Swan Lake*, the dance of the little swans is a perfect example of how precise ballet can be. Four dancers leap across the stage sideways, their arms linked together and their feet high and knees far apart as they perform *pas de chat*, or "step of the cat."

The little swans are supposed to move as one. They are

supposed to look as similar as possible, because otherwise the audience becomes distracted.

My skin was darker than the rest of the corps. And as Cindy had told me so long ago back in San Pedro, I had the perfect body for ballet according to George Balanchine. ABT's artistic director, Kevin McKenzie, agreed.

But no matter how talented I was or how hard I worked, some people would never believe I truly belonged in the world of professional ballet.

One day, ABT held an "open" rehearsal, which meant friends of the company could watch us, along with the people who donated money. During a quick break, an older man came over to talk to me. He was very direct when he spoke.

"You do realize you are the only black woman in the company, right?" he said. "And you very well could be the first to move beyond the corps in many decades."

He wasn't being mean. But he was the first person who'd ever mentioned my skin color the whole time I'd been at ABT.

We were preparing for tour, where our performances of *Swan Lake* would be filmed for television. I'd already performed the role of the four little swans during our spring season at the Metropolitan Opera House, but just a chance to dance as a swan in the corps de ballet would have been a dream. I'd be in an official film with ABT!

I'd been practicing hard, trying to perfect the dance of the four little swans that execute sixteen *pas de chat* in flawless rhythm.

Swan Lake is one of a group of ballets that include an act known as the "white act." Like *Giselle* and *La Bayadère*, the characters in the white act are ghosts and spirits. The dancers wear white and powder their skin to appear not human. One day, during a break from rehearsals, a friend approached me. She seemed uncomfortable.

She told me that she'd overheard some of the ABT staffers discussing *Swan Lake*. My name had come up, and it wasn't good. Someone didn't think I blended in with the rest of the dancers because of my brown skin. My stomach sank.

And then, when they announced who would be dancing the roles in the filmed production, my name wasn't on the list for the second act. The act that features the four little swans.

I knew that racism and bigotry existed. I couldn't forget the names my mother's ex-husband Robert had called my little sister, Lindsey, when we were growing up. I remembered how his family hadn't liked my siblings and me because of the African American blood in our heritage.

But I'd grown up in San Pedro, a place that celebrated all types of cultures. It was the home of Mexican, Russian, and Japanese immigrants, and so many of my neighbors and friends were of mixed-race backgrounds. I'd always known my brown skin made me different as a ballet dancer. But I didn't know anyone had thought of it as a problem.

Sometimes I had no choice but to look like the other dancers.

In the white ballets, dancers used white powder on their faces to transform into the ghosts and spirits they were playing. And when I danced those roles in ballets like *Giselle* and *Sylvia*, I had to use the same makeup. My skin was a beautiful brown, but I had to paint it white to match the rest of the corps. I had to lighten my skin.

It didn't bother me at first. I was so happy to be dancing with ABT in these classical roles. The makeup was unnatural, but it didn't seem like a big deal. It was part of the performance. But then the other dancers began to notice what I had to do to fit in. They began to make jokes about it.

"You're the only black girl, Misty," they would say,

laughing. "But you're always playing an animal that has to be white."

I giggled with them. Like the man who'd approached me at our rehearsal that day, I knew they weren't trying to be mean. But after a while, the joke stopped being funny.

Raven Wilkinson is now one of my mentors, but back in the 1950s, she was beginning her own career. In 1955, she became the first black American dancer to sign a full-time contract with a major ballet company. She joined the Ballet Russe de Monte Carlo, and she would regularly have to paint her already light skin white.

Now, nearly fifty years later, I had to do the same thing to be accepted as a professional ballet dancer.

chapter 17

I FELT ALONE AS A BLACK DANCER IN A professional company.

I work hard in rehearsals and performances, but that's not good enough for everyone. Some people still notice my skin color before they notice my talent. Others can't see past my complexion at all because they simply don't believe brown girls have a place in classical ballet.

But I wasn't the only one who had noticed there were so few women who look like me. In 2007, the *New York Times* printed a newspaper article titled "Where Are All the Black Swans?"

The article briefly mentioned me, pointing out that I was the only black woman dancing at ABT. It talked about the careers of a few different black women who'd come before me, including my mentor, Raven Wilkinson, who had faced extreme racism in the 1950s when she toured the United States with the Ballet Russe de Monte Carlo. The article also detailed the experiences of Tai Jimenez, who had been a principal with the Dance Theatre of Harlem and became its first member to join a major classical ballet company. Boston Ballet welcomed her as a principal in its ranks, but she'd been turned down by both the New York City Ballet and ABT.

Aesha Ash, whose breathtaking photo was included in the article, along with a picture of me performing with ABT principal Herman Cornejo, was interviewed. She spoke of when she had a family emergency and asked to take a break from her role in the corps of New York City Ballet. The artistic director told her he didn't think there was room for her to be promoted in the company and suggested she shouldn't return.

Then there was Alicia Graf Mack, who had also been rejected by ABT and New York City Ballet. She went on to dance with the Alvin Ailey American Dance Theater, a modern dance company started by a group of black American dancers.

I loved the article. I'd been a member of the ABT corps for six years when it was printed, and I felt like someone had read my mind. Black dancers were talking about how they didn't feel encouraged to join the classical ballet world. And that no matter how talented they were, they felt like no one wanted to see brown-skinned dancers in professional companies.

But as much as I liked not feeling so alone, I grew angry while reading the article. The experiences of Raven, Alicia, Tai, Aesha, and myself were all different, but they had one common thread: We didn't feel welcome, no matter how much we proved ourselves. That anger turned into determination. I still wanted to advance beyond the corps to become a soloist in the company, and then a principal.

And I would work as hard and as long as it took to make my dreams come true.

When I returned to ABT a couple of days after the article had been printed, one of my friends stopped me on my way to rehearsal.

"Did you see that stupid article in the *Times*, 'Where Are All the Black Swans?'" she asked. But she didn't sound like she'd read the same article. She sounded like she was offended. "What are they talking about? What a dumb story."

I was speechless. I couldn't believe what she'd just said. We danced and performed together week after week, and she didn't realize how I'd been feeling. She was my friend, but she didn't understand what I, or the few other black dancers who'd come before me, went through to dance in a professional company.

I had to walk away. I found an empty studio, closed myself inside, and began to cry. If my friends couldn't put themselves in my shoes, would anyone else? We all felt the various pressures of being professional dancers. We were expected to look a certain way and dance through the pain we felt from rigorous practice. We were expected to always look and be our best, even if that meant putting ourselves at risk of injury.

But the truth was that I faced extra pressure. I had to pretend like it didn't hurt when people judged my talent based on my skin color. I had to work extra hard to make sure they knew I deserved to be part of one of the best ballet companies in the world. And the worst part was there weren't any other black women in the company to talk to.

I couldn't share my frustrations and fears with anyone who truly understood.

There were some black men in the company. Not very many at one time—usually only one or two. And they'd move on after only a short stint with ABT. But I became friends with all of them: Danny, Jerry, Dante, and Jamar.

Eric Underwood was my best friend out of them all, though. We had so much in common. Like me, he'd grown up in a family that was tight-knit but didn't have a lot of money. He'd also come to ballet late, starting at fourteen. We liked all the same music growing up: mostly hip-hop and R & B. We'd go out for Red Lobster or BBQ, stuffing ourselves with ribs and burgers and shrimp.

I felt like myself around Eric. With him, I had not only a friend, but one who related to the experience of being a black dancer in a top ballet company. If someone said something offensive or racist, I didn't have to wonder if I was overreacting—or worse, if I'd imagined it. Eric would look over and I'd know he understood what I was feeling. We didn't even have to say anything.

One day, Kevin McKenzie called Eric into his office. Afterward, Eric pulled me aside to tell me what Kevin had said.

"He wants me to grow my hair long."

We laughed so hard we were crying.

Kevin's request might have seemed easy enough and probably wouldn't have meant anything to anyone else in the company. But Eric and I knew it meant Kevin, like so many other people, didn't understand the hair of people with African roots. Our coily hair grows out instead of down, so Eric had to explain that his hair would never be the type of "long" Kevin wanted, even if he didn't cut it short.

Laughing off these situations was the best way for Eric and me to deal with them. We were used to having to explain ourselves as black people—not just in life, but also in the incredibly white world of ballet. We knew we were expected to ignore the hurtful things that people said. Sometimes they were thoughtless comments. But other times they were purposely meant to hurt our feelings—to knock us down a peg and remind us we didn't really belong at ABT with everyone else.

I'm so grateful I had Eric in the company for as long as I did, but he eventually moved on. In addition to ABT, he's danced with the Dance Theatre of Harlem. He now lives in London, where he's currently a soloist with the Royal Ballet.

★ ★ ★ ★

While I generally felt alone at ABT and had trouble finding people in the company who understood my journey, I soon met women who offered support.

After a performance in Los Angeles, there was a note waiting for me on the pin board. The message was from a woman named Victoria Rowell, who wanted me to call her. She was an actress, and I couldn't believe she wanted to talk to me.

She invited me to her gorgeous home in the Hollywood Hills, sending a car to come get me. I'd only just met her, but we stayed up talking almost all night like old friends. Victoria has modeled and she became famous for her acting. She's been in dozens of movies and TV shows. Most people know her from the role she played on a soap opera, *The Young and the Restless*, for several years.

I was especially fascinated by the life that came before her fame. She'd grown up with foster parents and had loved ballet from a young age. Like me, she'd danced for some time with ABT's Studio Company. Although she didn't move on in her professional ballet career, I felt connected to her. Talking to her on that first evening, I thought, *There is actually someone out there I can relate to.*

Victoria was the first of many amazing women who came into my life and became a mentor to me.

Another woman who has been so important to me over the years is Susan Fales-Hill. Susan is biracial; her mother was a Haitian-American actress who worked on Broadway, and several centuries ago, her father's family arrived in the United States on the *Mayflower*. Susan is a writer and was a member of ABT's board of trustees, a group that makes decisions about how the company operates.

One day, Susan approached me. She could tell that I was struggling with my place in ABT.

"You know, many of our board members talk about you," she said, smiling at me. "They feel you are one of the most promising dancers in the company. That you have a future that is unbelievably bright. I agree."

Susan would go on to show her belief in me. Professional ballet dancers are sometimes sponsored by people who want to support the ballet. Each dancer/sponsor relationship is different, but in general, sponsors make sure we have everything we need to successfully rehearse and perform with the company. They guide us through the world of professional dance, and are often emotionally supportive, giving us someone to talk to whom we can trust.

Susan Fales-Hill became my sponsor, and I'm so appreciative that she took me under her wing. She encouraged me when I was feeling unsure about my future. She reminded me that my differences made me special and that I belonged at ABT. With her support, I was able to keep my eye on the prize and continue working toward my goals.

chapter 18

I KNEW I WAS LUCKY TO HAVE PEOPLE I could relate to. There was Eric, who always understood what I was thinking before I said anything. And Victoria Rowell and Susan Fales-Hill, who were kind and supportive, assuring me I wasn't completely alone in the all-white world of ballet.

But I still didn't feel like I was making any progress at ABT. I trained for eight hours a day, dancing until I was so tired I could barely stand. Yet no matter how hard I worked, I was afraid I wouldn't be able to advance in the company. I wasn't being cast in the classical roles that the other girls were considered for, though I had the grace and talent. And I worried that was solely because of my skin color.

I hadn't expected this. My mentors and instructors in California had believed in me and guided me when I was younger. But none of them had danced with a company as prestigious as ABT. I was older now, and instead of being the best in every class, I was simply a member of the corps. No one singled me out to demonstrate moves. I no longer had a Balanchine body.

I was so discouraged that I started to wonder if I should leave ABT.

I knew a dancer in the New York City Ballet. He said he would talk to the company's director and suggest he watch one of my performances. I thought that was a good idea. The New York City Ballet would be a fresh start, and maybe I would be more appreciated there.

Deep down, I think I knew that wasn't the right choice for me, though. I had no reason to think the New York City Ballet would want me. Back when I'd won the L.A. Spotlight Award, it had been the only company that didn't invite me to its summer intensive program. I couldn't forget the article in the *New York Times*, the one that said Aesha Ash had left the company after the director suggested she would never be promoted further than the corps.

But in the summer of 2004, I began to seriously consider another option.

That was the year I took a company class at the Dance Theatre of Harlem with Eric. Eric said the founder, Arthur Mitchell, wanted to meet me.

Arthur had a long career with the New York City Ballet. He joined in 1955 as the company's first black dancer, chosen by George Balanchine himself. He was promoted to principal during his fifteen years with the company. Balanchine choreographed roles just for Arthur, including the *pas de deux* in *Agon* and Puck in *A Midsummer Night's Dream*.

After the assassination of Martin Luther King Jr., Arthur was inspired to share his love of dance with the children in Harlem, where he'd grown up. He opened the Dance Theatre of Harlem in 1969, holding classes in a garage on 152nd Street.

I was familiar with the Dance Theatre of Harlem. And I had great respect for Arthur and the company. I'd been accepted to its summer program and offered a scholarship. The class we took with its company was exactly like the classes we took at ABT. And those, in a way, were just like the ones I'd taken at Cindy's and Diane's studios back in

Southern California. We started at the barre and moved on to center work. Only, in professional classes, the combinations were quicker and more complex. This was true at the Dance Theatre of Harlem, same as ABT.

Arthur watched me in the first class I took and during the *pas de deux* class I joined after that one. I wrote about meeting him in my journal:

He had a lot of good things to say about my dancing and his company, I scribbled excitedly across the page. *He reminded me of how special it is to be an African American ballerina. [He] said don't let them take you over. Walk into the room knowing you are the best. Shoulders back, chin up. Their attitudes will totally change.*

I would never forget that last sentiment: "Walk into a room, knowing you are somebody, somebody special. Don't ever let them smash that or pull you down."

I took another class at the Dance Theatre of Harlem two weeks later. The class was rigorous, and the other dancers were gifted and hardworking. I was used to both of those things at ABT. But I wasn't used to being in a roomful of so many other brown faces. Here, the staff wasn't concerned with how you looked—only how you danced.

After the class, Arthur told me he wanted me to be a

soloist in his company. Soloist, the position I'd been dreaming of since I'd joined ABT's Studio Company. I wrote more about talking to Arthur.

He said he was in the hospital a couple of years ago when he saw this girl on TV, I wrote. *She was sitting there with so much confidence, so much spark*, he said. *That was a ballerina.*

But now, Arthur said, he could tell something was different. I didn't have the same fire that he'd seen when he first watched me on television. He thought it was because of where I'd landed.

ABT had taken that from me, I continued writing in my journal. *I need that back. I need to always have that confidence inside the theater.*

I knew there was truth to what Arthur had said. My love for ballet had always shone through when I was dancing. That was what had been with me all these years, from my start at the Boys & Girls Club of San Pedro to Cindy's and Diane's dance studios to the Metropolitan Opera House here in New York City. My technique and talent were still there, but that fire had been extinguished.

Arthur reminded me of my roots. He said that as a black woman, that spark lived within me. "You have it. You can't be taught it," he told me.

Maybe it was time to move on from ABT. Arthur Mitchell believed in me. I wouldn't have to second-guess if I was being passed over for roles or promotions because of my brown skin. I would be able to dance lead roles in my beloved classical ballets, like *Cinderella* and *Sylvia* and *Giselle*. I felt wonderful hearing his praise; it was a welcome change from the negativity I could feel in the air around me at ABT.

But then, just as I was imagining myself as a soloist at the Dance Theatre of Harlem, I thought of my mother.

I'd spent my whole childhood moving from place to place, from Mommy's ex-husbands to her new boyfriends. Sometimes those moves were good for us, like when we'd left Robert. But that feeling of relief usually didn't last long. We'd end up somewhere worse or with someone we disliked even more, and what we'd just left didn't seem so bad after all.

I couldn't become my mother, running away when things were tough. It was a bad pattern, and I didn't want to repeat her mistakes.

I told Arthur I appreciated the offer, but I had to stay at ABT.

It didn't take long to see that I'd made the right decision.

The Dance Theatre of Harlem shut down later that year because of money troubles. The main company didn't take the stage again until almost ten years later.

I went back to my journal to write about ABT: *I need to go in there and show them how good I am.*

I wasn't ready to stop fighting my way to the top at ABT. Maybe I'd have to work ten times harder than anyone else because of my skin color, because I didn't have the body they thought was ideal for ballet. If that's what it took to become a principal dancer, I'd keep pushing myself.

I couldn't stop now. I'd given up so much to get here. I'd make them see that I deserved it—and more.

chapter 19

DESPITE THE DISAPPOINTMENT AND
frustration I felt at ABT, I loved living in New York City.

In the ballet studio, where I spent most of my time, I
was the only one: the only brown face in a sea of whiteness.
Anyone who walked in the room would immediately pick
me out as the dancer who was different.

But out in the bustling city, I couldn't walk more than a
few feet without seeing people who looked like me. People
of mixed ancestry, with golden-brown skin and curvy bodies. I blended in with everyone on the street, and no one
who looked at me thought I had the wrong body or the
wrong skin color. I was just one of them.

I talked to people of all different backgrounds who

thought I was one of them when they first met me: Puerto Rican, Dominican, East Indian. I couldn't claim their foods and accents and history as my own, but around them, I felt like I belonged.

It had taken a while for me to get used to the city. The warm, dry weather of Southern California had been replaced by the thick, heavy humidity of New York City summers. The city was gritty and constantly pulsing, full of life, while California had been slower and more relaxed. Even little things, like the shoes I wore, changed. The flip-flops I'd been so quick to slip on back home were defense-less against the grimy streets of New York.

After living with Isabel Brown my first two years in the city, I moved out on my own. And I quickly learned that in New York City, you had to pay extra to have windows and natural light in your apartment. When I moved out of Isabel's brownstone, my friends and I christened my first place "the dungeon." The windows had bars on the outside of them, and they didn't let in any light because they were just a few feet away from a brick wall.

But I loved living in New York, and explored it end-lessly. I ate yassa chicken, a dish from Senegal, with my friend Leyla in Harlem. We wandered through Central

Park and went shopping in SoHo. I bought cheap tickets to Broadway shows, visited street fairs, and went out dancing with friends. I felt so free, dancing without worrying that someone didn't think I was good enough . . . or that I didn't look the part.

I met lots of new people in New York, but I connected with one person in particular. His name was Olu, and we met through mutual friends. He was working at a law firm in the city for the summer. I liked him instantly. He was handsome—his skin was a warm caramel brown—and he had a gentle, kind spirit. Like me, he was of mixed-race ancestry: His mother was Jewish and his father was black. Eventually, he became my husband.

He had to return to law school in Atlanta shortly after we met, but we kept in touch over the next year. We talked on the phone and texted often. Every few months, he'd visit me in the city, taking quick breaks from his studies. Once he graduated, he moved to New York and began working as a lawyer.

Olu has been supportive of me and my career since we first met. I was open with him about the troubles I'd had at ABT. How I was worried I wouldn't be promoted. How I feared that my dreams would be squashed before I was given the chance to prove myself.

He suggested some changes that might help. "Eat fish tonight instead of beef," he would say. Or, since he worked out, he would give advice on the type of exercises I should do. Through Olu, I realized I didn't have to make huge changes to my diet or workouts to fit the mold ABT required. I could compromise by making small changes.

"ABT is still excited about you," Olu said when I was feeling down. "They still see a future with you. You just have to work on this one little thing."

And it always helped to know that in Olu's eyes, I was beautiful just the way I was.

I didn't like speaking up. I liked pleasing people, and I didn't want to hurt anyone's feelings or make them angry with me. But Olu taught me that I had to stand up for myself if I wanted to achieve my dreams. As a black woman, I knew that I had to work ten times harder than white people just to get what they had. As a lawyer, he knew that sometimes working your hardest wasn't enough. Sometimes you had to use your words.

He helped me practice what I would discuss with Kevin, ABT's artistic director. I would take notes about what I wanted to say. Then I would pretend we were in Kevin's office, and Olu would temporarily turn into Kevin.

"I want to be pushed," I would say, my voice shaking as I looked down at my notes. "I want to be a classical dancer. I'm a strong member of the company and can play those roles. And I want to give everything to this company. I appreciate the opportunity you've given me, and I want you to trust me, to believe in me."

Olu would pretend to be Kevin: "But you're so wonderful with the contemporary works. You shone in *Gong*. We have modern choreographers who want to create works just for you. Why not focus on those?"

"I know contemporary is a strength of mine," I'd reply, my confidence growing. My voice stopped shaking. "But I want to be a *ballerina*."

I was so scared of speaking up that I *had* to read from the note cards. I cared so much about ballet. Dance had changed my life. It had allowed me to get through the hard times of my childhood, when I was moving from place to place with Mommy and all of my siblings. Ballet had been an escape from the embarrassment of my mother's constantly changing boyfriends and husbands. Gracefully leaping across the studio in a *grand jeté* soothed the pain I still felt when I thought of how I'd had to break ties with Cindy.

Talking about how much I loved ballet made me

nervous. I didn't like looking so weak in front of my boy-friend. But Olu didn't give up on me. He was sweet and helpful.

"You can do this," he would reassure me. "They picked *you*. Just remind them of all you can do."

Just like the rehearsals before a big performance, practicing with Olu gave me strength. It stripped away my nerves and helped me focus on *what* I needed to say—not the fact that I needed to say something in the first place. Preparing to talk to Kevin, I also remembered that ABT wouldn't have offered me a contract if they didn't believe I was talented. It was one of the most respected ballet companies in the world, and I was dancing in its corps. If I left now, how long would it be before another woman of color was given this chance?

With my confidence boosted, I told Kevin I needed to talk to him. We met in his office.

"I know contemporary ballet is a strength of mine because a lot of ballerinas don't move like I do," I said. "But I was trained as a classical dancer, and that's what I really want to do."

"I'm glad to hear that," Kevin said. "You have the talent to do both."

I was pleased to finally know that he believed in me and gave me the opening to start going for the more classical roles. And when I looked back, I thought that maybe he'd supported me more than I'd realized.

Kevin's job as artistic director isn't easy. He has to handle business affairs for the company while maintaining relationships with the dancers he's chosen. He has to make difficult decisions, like firing dancers who aren't performing well enough. He tells us when we're doing a good job, but he also has to be tough on us if we aren't dancing to our strongest potential.

My relationship with Kevin has changed over the years. I was only a teenager when he met me. I've grown since then, and the way I've looked at him has shifted too. At first he was like one of my teachers in school—someone I wanted to impress because I respected him so much. Then I saw him as a mentor, someone who encouraged me to do my best and helped me work through the obstacles of my career. Now I've been dancing under his direction for more than a decade, and our relationship has changed again.

I still have great respect for him, but before he was an artistic director, Kevin was a dancer, like me. He's still a dancer, and now I view him as someone I can talk to, the way I talk to the other dancers in the company: my colleagues.

One of my favorite parts of being in ABT is after we perform, when the curtains have just closed. Kevin and the other ballet mistresses and masters don't watch our shows from backstage. They observe us from a box in the theater. But immediately after the show, Kevin is waiting for us with comments about our performance.

"This is what you did wrong during the coda," he'll say to one of the principal dancers. Or he'll tell another person, "For the next show, make sure you enter a beat sooner."

He doesn't have time to give notes to all of us. There are eighty dancers in the company, and sometimes there are so many of us onstage at once that it's hard to focus on everyone. But Kevin and his staff are always trying to help us be the best dancers we can. Getting their critiques after each show is a long tradition, and I miss it when we're between seasons.

Thinking about all the years I've spent dancing in Kevin's company, I understand now that even when I didn't feel like ABT supported me, he's always shown his belief in me.

In 2002, shortly after I'd come back to New York, healed from my back injury, Kevin said he wanted me to compete as an ABT dancer in one of the most important dance competitions in the world.

Kevin nominated a dancer each year to compete for the Princess Grace Foundation scholarships and apprenticeships. The foundation gives out these prizes to young people competing in the film, theater, and dance categories. That year, I would represent ABT.

It was proof that Kevin had faith in my talent. I'd been gone a year, recovering from my injury, and he'd still chosen me. Entering the competition was also a way to regain the confidence I'd lost being away from ABT for so long. The company would film my performance and send it in to the foundation for consideration.

We decided I would dance the *pas de deux* from *Tarantella*. It's a famous ballet choreographed by George Balanchine in 1964. My partner was Craig Salstein. We were old friends from ABT's summer intensive, and then the Studio Company. He'd been my first partner, and when we were both members of the main company's corps, we danced the peasant *pas de deux* from *Giselle*.

Tarantella was an innovative ballet, especially for the classical world. The steps varied from big, sweeping leaps to fast footwork *en pointe*. The movements were fun to

The Copeland clan (*clockwise from top left*):
Doug Jr., Chris, Erica, and me

LEFT: My very first time *en pointe*, which Cindy was confident (and quick) enough to capture on film. RIGHT: A *pas de deux* class at Cindy's studio. In the background, you can see Jason—this was one of the days he decided to come to class.

Dancing with Ashley Ellis. This was from my first
week at Lauridsen, when we were so fascinated
by our similarities. We were like sisters—at ABT,
they called her "the white Misty."
INSET: The Bradleys and me. Proof that I was
never different to them, just a part of the family.

Lola's warm heart. She was so nurturing
and natural in her affection from the start.

I was photographed during my ABT audition. In the
background, you can see Jared Matthews and Craig
Salstein, both of whom are also now soloists!

Soul mates. Leyla and I were inseparable.

Eric—my brother at ABT

My family. *Top row:* Miranda and Tom (the Cantines' daughter-in-law and son); *middle row:* Lindsey, Jeff (Erica's husband), me, Aiden Cantine (the Cantines' grandson), Sofie Cantine (the Cantines' granddaughter), Erica, Mariah, Mom; *bottom row:* Liz, Chris

With my father, Doug, in Chicago

Olu

Legendary ballerina and mentor Raven Wilkinson and me in my apartment, after interviewing her for a documentary

As the Firebird, with Herman Cornejo
INSET: In the ABT costume shop, being fitted for my Firebird headpiece

Back where I started—with a group of talented
young dancers from the Boys & Girls Club

Onstage as an odalisque in *Le Corsaire*.
I've danced this role ever since
I joined the company.

execute. Both Craig and I held tambourines that jingled as we touched them to our hands and feet.

I also performed a piece from *Don Quixote.*

Trying to pick a favorite ballet is nearly impossible. We love them all because we love dance. We like to watch the more complex ballets being performed by our heroes, and we love to be onstage ourselves, tackling the complicated technique.

But the truth is that you always feel more connected to certain ballets than others. *Don Quixote* had been special to me since I first discovered ballet, watching Gelsey Kirkland in the ABT videos so long ago at Cindy's house. I'd performed it at Cindy's school—my first full-length ballet—and it was the first ballet I'd seen Paloma Herrera perform, back in L.A. I'd also auditioned for the L.A. Spotlight Awards with a piece from *Don Quixote*—and won.

I didn't win the Princess Grace Foundation prize. But competing for such a prestigious award was another achievement in my career. And I felt proud that Kevin had chosen me to represent ABT.

chapter 20

WHEN WE WERE KIDS, MY SIBLINGS AND I were never quite sure why Mommy had left our father back in Kansas City. She had told us she wasn't happy with him. We knew that much. And over the years, we saw her pick up and leave so often that moving became common. We didn't think to ask what had made her leave that first time or why we never spoke to our father again.

I hadn't missed my father. When I was really young, I had my mother's second husband, Harold. And even though his relationship with my mother didn't work out, he'd been an attentive, caring father to me and my siblings. Her next husband, Robert, had been kind to me, and seemed like a father, in a way—even though my memories are clouded by how horrible he was to my brothers and my baby sister, Lindsey.

But as I got older, I started to wonder about my father, Doug Copeland. And I wasn't the only one.

When I was sixteen and beginning to seriously study ballet, my brother Doug Jr. said he wanted to meet our father. This wasn't such a surprise, looking back. Doug had always been interested in where we came from—as a family and as African Americans. Once, when I was in third grade, he was sitting on the porch after school, picking at something small and white.

"What are you doing?" I asked.

"I'm reading about our history—about slavery—and I wanted to know what it felt like for our ancestors," he said. "So I'm picking cotton."

Doug was named after our father, so maybe that's why his interest in reconnecting with him was stronger. A few months after he said he was going to search for his name-sake, he told me he'd found him.

"He's living in Wisconsin," Doug said excitedly. "I tracked him down, and we've been talking on the phone. I'm going to get some money together and go see him."

I liked seeing Doug so happy, but I still didn't think

about meeting our father. Not even after my brother went to visit him and came back with fun stories and photos. Not even after I saw how much we looked like him.

I started to think about my father again after I'd been dancing in the corps for two years. I wondered if he knew about me and my career as a ballerina. I wondered what his voice sounded like, and I wondered if he had missed my siblings and me after we left him. I couldn't stop thinking about him. Finally, I called Doug Jr. and said I wanted to meet our father too.

We booked tickets to Wisconsin, and I met my dad on August 20, 2004. He looked a little nervous when he first said hello to me, but then he gave me a big hug. He was sweet, telling stories about growing up in Kansas City and about when he first met my mother. He said he'd loved her and that he'd loved us, too, even when we were so far away. He said he was proud of us.

I was on a break from ABT and able to stay in Wisconsin for a week. I was also able to spend time with my great-aunt and some of my cousins. I'd never met any of them.

I have his lips, I wrote about my father in my journal. *I wish I had his pretty hazel eyes. That would look fresh on me.*

It's like a part of me has been fulfilled. I'm really happy.

My father had been in a relationship with a woman named Debbie for many years, but he never had more children. As kids, Mommy had never told us not to look for him. But somehow, we'd always known she didn't want us talking to him after we left. Meeting my father and listening to him talk, I understood that he had never wanted to cut ties with us. He had never stopped loving us. He was hurt that our mother left and took their four children with her.

I met my father more than ten years ago, and we're still getting to know each other. Sometimes it seems like we should have been able to jump right into our relationship as father and daughter. But we've been separated for more years than we've known each other. It takes time to build any relationship.

He's trying. When ABT travels to Chicago to perform, he'll come down with Debbie from Wisconsin to watch me. And we have a standing phone date. Every Sunday morning at ten, my father calls to catch up with his youngest daughter.

I felt like a new person after I met my father and returned to New York.

I was ready to prove that I deserved to be promoted to soloist. If I were promoted, I'd be the first black soloist at

ABT in nearly twenty years. I felt good about my career. Inspired. I knew that I had to be driven to get what I wanted. I had to work hard on my technique and turn out flawless performances. My goal felt like it was actually within reach. And if I met that goal, next I could focus on becoming a principal.

If this could open doors for black women in ballet, that would mean the world to me, I penned in my diary. *It would all be worth it. That's what I'm doing this for. Not for my own pleasure and gratification. I need to remember this every morning I wake up tired, just think[ing] of what I could do, not just for me but [for] others.*

chapter 21

ONE MORNING, I WOKE UP TO A TEXT FROM
my friend Kaylen Ratto. We'd become fast friends back in
California, at the Lauridsen Ballet Centre, and traveled to
New York to attend summer intensives—Kaylen at the
Joffrey and me at ABT.

Can I give Prince your cell number? she texted me.

Prince? As in Prince, the legendary musician?

Kaylen said a person who worked for Prince had called
her office to ask how to reach me. Kaylen was working for
a company called Career Transition for Dancers. The office
helps dancers find new jobs where they can use their ballet
skills after they retire.

I couldn't say yes fast enough. But I had no idea why Prince would want to talk to me.

My phone rang that afternoon. I instantly recognized his voice. Lots of people would give up everything to talk to Prince, but I didn't feel much of anything when he spoke. I knew it was a big deal to talk to someone as famous and as talented as him. But I mostly just wanted to know why he was calling.

I had, of course, heard his songs on the radio and watched his music videos on MTV. I'd seen his movie *Purple Rain*. But he wasn't one of my favorite musicians. I usually listened to R & B and hip-hop and boy bands.

Prince had a deep voice, but he was soft-spoken. "I'm remaking a song, 'Crimson and Clover,' and I would love to have you in the video."

I started thinking of his music. I couldn't exactly picture myself dancing to it, but I was curious. And flattered that he wanted to collaborate with me.

"That would be *awesome*," I said to Prince.

Both Mommy and Olu thought working with Prince sounded like an amazing opportunity. And I had the time. ABT was on a break. I agreed to be in the video.

Prince flew me out to Los Angeles—first class. My family was in the area, but Prince had arranged for me to stay at the incredibly fancy Beverly Hills Hotel. I had a huge, luxurious suite all to myself. When I arrived at the hotel, I was greeted with champagne, flowers, and a note from Prince. I was taken around town in a limousine.

I didn't meet Prince until the next day. I was at the video shoot, getting my makeup done, when he came over. He was quiet and didn't act like a super-famous celebrity. He shook my hand, and he seemed shy when he met me.

Prince trusted me to choreograph my own dance. I listened to the music and created right on the set as he watched.

That night, I went to his home for dinner. The limousine picked me up from the hotel. When I slid into the backseat, there was a present waiting for me. The wrapping was gorgeous. Inside, I found the beautiful designer gown I had worn during the video shoot earlier that day.

When I got to his house, Prince wasn't ready. I walked around the main rooms, admiring his purple piano and the big, long windows that started at the ceiling and ended at the floor. His private chef made us a vegan meal, and we ate at one of the longest dining tables I've ever seen.

Prince respected my art and wanted to know everything about me. He asked all about my life, from what type of music I liked to my career with ABT.

I went back to my hotel after dinner, but it wouldn't be the last time I saw Prince.

He called every once in a while, and I saw him again about a year after we'd first met at the video shoot. He invited me to a concert in New York. I took a car to meet him, and we watched the performance away from the crowd. It was a funk group called Graham Central Station, and Prince played guitar with them at one point during the show. I loved watching him perform. He was incredibly talented, and the audience adored him.

I didn't hear from him again until almost six months later. I never knew why he was calling. This time he wanted to collaborate again. "I'm going on tour in Europe," he said. "I'd love for you to be a part of some of the shows. You could maybe even kick it off with a solo."

I hadn't had to ask permission to do the video shoot with him when ABT was on hiatus. But when we were performing or rehearsing for our upcoming seasons, I had to put in a formal request to do anything outside of ABT. Most of the time, those requests are not approved.

I was lucky: The tour wouldn't begin until later in the summer. I could go.

I couldn't believe I was going on tour with Prince. He

was such a gifted, respected musician. But more than that, I would be dancing in front of people who may not be familiar with ballet. I'd be introducing ballet to a mainstream audience.

I met Prince in Paris. He picked me up from Charles de Gaulle Airport, and the driver took us to the Hôtel Le Bristol. We went to a concert the first night: singer-songwriter Erykah Badu. She was wonderful. After her show, Erykah and I watched Prince perform at a party for hours. He was serious about his art, rehearsing as much as I did before a performance.

The show in Paris was canceled, but we moved on to Nice, France, and then Cannes. At the show, Prince's band and background singers went out onstage first. Then it was my turn. I hadn't practiced what I would do, but I knew my technique and love of ballet would shine through. This was a concert, not the studios or stages of ABT. No one would be staring to make sure my form was perfect.

I danced for a couple of minutes. I had just swept my leg forward and up from my hip, so high that it almost kissed my forehead. Then I brought it back down in a straight line, quick but controlled. A *grand battement*. The audience began screaming.

Wow, I thought. *They liked that!*

But then, out of the corner of my eye, I saw Prince had arrived. Obviously the cheers were for him. I danced off the stage and watched from the wings. I knew Prince as a quiet, sweet, humble friend. But this was *the* Prince. The performer who had made a name for himself decades ago. He was fierce and filled with energy that crackled through the giant crowd of fans. I'd always admired him, but I especially did in that moment.

After the tour, I didn't see him again until about a year later. It was fall 2011. I flew out to Minnesota, where he lived, to do a photo shoot. He also wanted to talk about collaborating again, but I didn't know any details until I arrived in Minnesota.

Prince was going on tour again, this time in the United States. He hadn't toured for American audiences in a long time; he was going to call it Welcome to America. The first show would be at Madison Square Garden, in my home of New York City. I felt special that he wanted to collaborate with me before the shows even started. For this tour, he wanted me to dance a piece that would be choreographed specifically for the show.

I had to pull double duty, working with Prince. ABT

was rehearsing for *The Nutcracker*. We'd be performing at the Brooklyn Academy of Music, but we had to rehearse at a theater in New Jersey during the day.

My schedule was so full! I'd practice with the company from ten o'clock in the morning until nine o'clock at night. A choreographer would come to the theater when I had breaks and we'd rehearse the pieces I was going to dance at the concert. After finishing rehearsals at ABT, I'd take a limousine that Prince sent for me and meet him at the Izod Center in New Jersey. We practiced very late—usually until two o'clock in the morning. I'd loved the freedom I had to create my own choreography in the shows during his European tour. But I appreciated how Prince wanted a specific type of dance. I was used to that, having been with ABT for so long.

Prince gave me and the choreographer notes after each rehearsal. My dance was to "The Beautiful Ones," a song from the *Purple Rain* album that had also been in the movie. I listened to the song on repeat. Prince wanted to be sure I knew every single lyric and the musical cues I'd be following.

I felt at the top of my game when I was collaborating with Prince. His faith in me made me feel like I was finally a professional. I felt like I was in charge of my career, being celebrated for what I do best by such a successful artist. I felt like a true ballerina.

Performing outside of ABT gave me confidence. Within the company, I always worried that if I messed up in rehearsal, I'd jeopardize my chances of being cast in important roles. When I was dancing without the pressure of ABT, I could concentrate on the art of ballet itself—and how much I loved it.

I didn't dance with Prince for every show on his tour in the States. Because ABT was performing *The Nutcracker* at the same time, I had to miss some of the concerts. He simply cut out my piece from the show on the nights I was with ABT, dancing in Brooklyn.

I was especially nervous the night of the first concert, at Madison Square Garden. While Prince was performing, I slipped below the stage to a small room he used to change between musical sets. After playing a couple of songs, he came downstairs and stood next to me. He hugged me.

"Let's do it," he said.

He was lifted back up to the stage from a small platform. It was supposed to drop back down and I would step onto it and come up to the stage the same way Prince had.

Only it didn't drop back down.

Oh no, I thought, anxiety washing over me. *That's my cue! I'm supposed to be onstage!*

Finally, the platform lowered. It had been only a few seconds, but it seemed like it had taken forever.

Up onstage, I walked over to meet Prince at his piano and prepared to begin the dance we'd practiced over and over again in rehearsals.

Prince stopped singing just before I started my solo.

"Ladies and gentlemen, Misty Copeland!" he announced me.

My heart was beating so fast. I hadn't known he was going to do that. I felt proud when he acknowledged me as a guest artist. I wasn't just a background dancer to him. It felt like we were partners in the performance.

The moves weren't very complicated. I was wearing the same gown from the "Crimson and Clover" video, but the dress was two sizes too big. The long train that trailed behind me weighed me down too much to jump or do more than simple turns. The stage wasn't the kind I was used to dancing on; the floor didn't have the proper support for the pointe shoes I was wearing. I danced on the piano, spinning across the top in *piqué* and *chaîné* turns.

I performed with Prince at Madison Square Garden a few more times, as well as at the Forum in L.A. I cherish those memories of working with him on that tour.

Prince was a fan of the ballet, and he came to watch me perform many times. I loved knowing he was in the audience. He believed in my dancing and made me feel like I belonged at ABT. He reminded me of Arthur Mitchell when he told me I didn't need to be so humble about my talent. "You are a queen, a diva in the best way," he would tell me.

He was one of the best in his field, and knowing he thought I was a special dancer changed the way I thought about myself and my career.

ABT had been wonderful as my career progressed. The staff was kind to let me have the time off to rehearse and perform with Prince. They didn't have to say yes. But they showed how much they believed in me within ABT, too, which meant so much to me. And when I thought back to the start of my career, I understood the company had always supported me.

Once, Elaine Kudo, who was the first to partner with Mikhail Baryshnikov in *Push Comes to Shove*, one of Twyla Tharp's most famous ballets, approached me. She said how much she admired my performance in *The Eyes That Gently Touch*, a contemporary piece I'd danced the year before. I was so flattered when she told me that my performance had been her favorite out of the three companies she'd watched perform the ballet.

Another time, David Richardson, who was the artistic assistant director of ABT then, said he'd been talking to John Meehan the day before. John was the artistic director of ABT's Studio Company, where I had started. He'd also danced with the main company as a principal.

"I'm very excited about this upcoming season," John had told David. When David asked why, John said, "Because there's going to be a Misty Copeland . . ."

John had praised my talent to David. It felt so good to know that he was looking forward to watching me dance. It made me feel like I was appreciated at ABT.

I was so happy, so lighthearted. I felt like I could dance on air.

chapter 22

I FELT BUOYED BY THE SUPPORT AND mentorship I received from Kevin McKenzie and ABT, and my confidence soared when I was able to step outside of the company and flex my talent with other performers, like Prince.

But I felt even more complete as a dancer, as a woman of color working in a very white profession, when I learned about the black ballerinas who had graced the stage before me.

Before that *New York Times* article had been published, the first time I ever heard Raven Wilkinson's name was when I watched a documentary on the Ballet Russe de Monte Carlo. I couldn't believe I'd never heard of this talented, beautiful, and groundbreaking dancer who was the first African American woman to join a major ballet company. She should have been a household name, but instead I was only just learning of her. Many of my fellow dancers didn't know about her either.

But better late than never. I learned all about the difficulty Raven had faced when she was dancing with the Ballet Russe. While touring the Southern United States in the 1950s, Raven was threatened with violence multiple times by the Ku Klux Klan, a terrorist group that believed in white supremacy. Raven wasn't safe traveling to certain parts of the country, so she was, unfortunately, forced to leave the company. She eventually moved to Holland and danced with the Dutch National Ballet for several years.

I was fascinated and inspired by how Raven had survived such difficult times. I talked about her a lot. After my manager, Gilda Squire, did some research, we learned that Raven was still alive. Not only that, but she lived in New York City, just a couple of blocks from my apartment on the Upper West Side!

When Gilda talked to her, Raven said she knew all about me and my career. Raven Wilkinson had watched my interviews on TV and read articles written about me.

She was just as interested in me as I was in her. That felt incredible, to have made an impact on someone I respected so much.

Gilda decided we should do an event together. I would have a conversation with Raven at the Studio Museum in Harlem. We had spoken before the event, in a radio interview to promote our public conversation. We only talked over the phone then, but I was so moved just hearing her speak. When we met in Harlem, we hugged and I immediately started crying.

We still talk today. Raven is always in the audience at my performances, and many times we'll go out to dinner afterward. She is one of my greatest supporters, always reminding me of how far I can go. And she understands a life that very few do: the life of a black classical ballet dancer.

As a black ballerina with such a prestigious company, I think it's my responsibility to talk about the African American dancers who came before me. Raven's path allowed me to advance to where I am today. It's important to recognize all the black dancers who have made their mark on the ballet world but weren't always given the respect they deserved: Aesha Ash, Alicia Graf Mack, Lauren Anderson, Tai Jimenez, and more.

Succeeding in ballet is about talent, of course. But it is also dependent on money and luck. I benefited from one of those. I've had a wonderful career filled with support and guidance from people and places I could never have imagined. But there were times when it was difficult, when I would have given anything to see someone in class or onstage who looked like me. Although I may be the only one at ABT, I'm comforted by the fact that Aesha and Tai and Raven were able to pave the way.

Sometimes my fellow dancers thought ignoring my race was better than acknowledging our differences. I would confide in them at times, talking about how I felt like I was being passed over for classical roles or how some people didn't think I belonged onstage with the rest of the company.

"But we don't think of you as black," they'd say. They thought that would make me feel better. They thought I just wanted to blend in. But those words bothered me. And I wondered, *Well, how do you see black people in general if you believe* not *thinking of me that way is a compliment?*

Still, my confidence was growing. I threw myself into rehearsals and performances, giving my all.

A few years ago, we were performing *Sleeping Beauty*, and I was dancing the part of Puss in Boots. The makeup for the role was white powder. The makeup artist was standing next to me, prepared to apply it to my face.

"I don't understand why the cats have to be white," I said, looking at her. "I want to be a brown cat."

So I danced as a brown cat.

In 2007, I represented ABT in another competition. The competitors were all members of the four best ballet companies in the world—ABT, the Royal Ballet, the National Ballet of Canada, and the Royal Danish Ballet. Kevin McKenzie nominated me, along with Jared Matthews, another dancer in the corps, to compete for the Erik Bruhn Prize in Canada.

I was thrilled for the opportunity to compete and prove that Kevin should continue to have faith in me. I felt comfortable knowing I would dance with Jared; we'd partnered together often.

I injured my foot practicing jumps three days before the competition. ABT would be performing *Swan Lake* on tour after the Erik Bruhn Prize, and I was rehearsing the part of the jumping girl in *Swan Lake*. The doctor told me I had a stress reaction in a group of bones called meta-tarsal. I rested the next day, hoping I'd be better with a little time off.

There was a surprise when I returned and entered my dressing room. A suitcase I didn't recognize was planted in the middle of the room. I hadn't spoken to anyone about what would happen if I couldn't compete. But that suitcase was the only message I needed. It was obvious that there was someone else ready to take my spot if I couldn't work through the pain. I couldn't let that happen—I would go to Canada.

For the competition, we performed the *grand pas de deux* from *Sleeping Beauty*. I had danced the piece several times when I was part of the Studio Company. Jared and I also performed a variation from a contemporary ballet by Jirí Kylián. I was anxious about representing ABT in such a prestigious competition. I'd been fighting so hard to dance classical roles that I felt like I had to do my very best at the *Sleeping Beauty* performance.

Jared and I didn't win, but I left Canada knowing I'd performed to my best ability.

Just a few weeks later, I received a prize that I'd been working toward for years: Kevin McKenzie promoted me to soloist at ABT. He'd been with us the night of the Erik Bruhn Prize and said it was the first time I looked like a true ballerina.

I was making history. There hadn't been a black female soloist at ABT in two decades.

I didn't cry tears of joy when Kevin called me into his office, even though I'd been waiting to hear those words since I was a teenager. I was unbelievably happy that I'd achieved my dream after six years with ABT, but I also knew how hard I had worked for it. And I was so happy that I'd finally proven myself to Kevin, who'd chosen me to represent the company in such an important competition.

I'd worried for so long that I didn't belong, and now I was sure that I was exactly where I was supposed to be.

No matter how many dreams I'd accomplished, I never forgot where I came from.

In 2011, I was honored to film a commercial for the Boys & Girls Clubs of America. I owed my love of ballet to the Boys & Girls Club in San Pedro. And in recording the public service announcement, I joined so many other celebrities whose lives had been impacted by the organization: Denzel Washington, Jennifer Lopez, Kerry Washington,

Cuba Gooding Jr., Smokey Robinson, Magic Johnson, and Sugar Ray Leonard, to name a few.

I was able to chat with the commercial's cast between takes. It felt like we were all old friends—maybe because we'd all been "club kids" growing up. Denzel even had a connection to ABT! Many years ago, before his career had taken off, he'd been a curtain boy at the Metropolitan Opera House. Once, he pulled the curtain for an ABT performance starring Natalia Makarova and Mikhail Baryshnikov! I also loved talking to Kerry, who told me how much she supported me and my career.

The next year, I was inducted into the Boys & Girls Club Alumni Hall of Fame in San Diego.

I was surrounded by the people who'd helped shape my childhood: Elizabeth and Dick Cantine, Mommy, and even the Bradleys. I had seen Cindy and Patrick a few times over the years, but the Boys & Girls Club asked if it was okay to invite them. Everyone knew about the drama that had surrounded my family and Cindy's so many years ago. And this would be the first time all of us had been in the same room together since then. But of course I wanted Cindy there. And I made sure to thank her in my speech. I had come so far because of her early belief in my talent.

I was proud to be recognized by the Boys & Girls Club. I was happy to make my speech and so thrilled that finally, all of the people who had been such an integral part of my younger years could be in one room to celebrate. There was no arguing or tension—just happiness.

chapter 23

I USED TO BE TERRIFIED OF DISAPPOINTING
people. When I was younger, I couldn't think of anything
worse than disobeying the rules, making someone mad, or
failing someone when they were counting on me. This was
true at school, where I liked making sure my fellow students
showed up to class before the bell rang. It was also true at
home, where I refused to complain aloud about Mommy
and her boyfriends like my siblings did.

I didn't like being judged, but as a professional ballet
dancer, I am constantly in the spotlight. I am always being
judged—often by people I will never meet. And each time
I set foot onstage, whether it's at the Brooklyn Academy of

Music or the Metropolitan Opera House, I face the possibility of disappointing someone.

After so many years striving to make it to the top at ABT, I knew that I had support from so many people: my mother, Kevin McKenzie, and the various mentors and dancers who had come into my life. But knowing I was backed by all those people who believed in me didn't always make it easy to ignore those who were critical of me and my career.

There were the bloggers who were upset that I talked about race within the ballet world. They accused me of "playing the race card." Then there were the ones who believed a true ballerina wouldn't have danced onstage with a pop star like Prince—they found my performance at his concerts "demeaning." Other blogs complained that I did too many interviews and craved the spotlight offstage too much.

I didn't like reading the criticism, but sometimes I was just too curious to stay away. And I hoped that, ultimately, I would get to a place where I wouldn't be bothered at all by the opinions of strangers. But the truth was that reading the blogs made me angry and upset.

As I got to know Paloma Herrera, I learned that she doesn't read reviews about her performances. Sometimes I wish I could stay away from them too. She doesn't have to worry about being judged by people who have never seen her perform and never shaken her hand.

I don't have the time or opportunity to talk to everyone in person, so being online is a great way to chat with my fans. I enjoy the connections we can make through social media. It allows me to talk to longtime ballet fans or those who have discovered ballet by watching videos of me online. Some people think I'm taking advantage of my position as a professional ballerina. Instead, I like to think that the more interviews I give and the more I perform outside of ABT, the more people will relate to ballet—especially young people.

People also have a lot to say about my heritage. I've always stood out as a black dancer surrounded by blond-haired, blue-eyed ballerinas. Often, I have been *the* black dancer—the only one in a company of dozens. But when I talk about how I succeeded despite starting ballet when I was older and growing up poor, people want to ignore the black genes in my blood.

I am the person living this life, and I identify as a black woman. I'm proud of my African American roots, culture, and features. Defining myself as black is not "playing a card," and I will not feel bad for speaking up about the prejudice and racism that still exists in the ballet world. Things are much better for me than they were for all of the Raven Wilkinsons who have come before me. I hope that by talking about these issues, professional ballet will be an even better experience for all the little brown girls who strive to succeed at this art form. I dance for them. And if I've helped just one little girl realize her dream when I'm leaping across the stage, then all of the hard work and difficult times have been worth it.

No matter what anyone else thought, I knew how much I'd overcome to achieve my success. And I knew that I couldn't let their words get to me. I had to keep working, keep pushing through the obstacles that were put in my way.

The Firebird is a ballet with music composed by Igor Stravinsky. It tells the story of Prince Ivan, who becomes lost in a magical garden, where he meets and traps the gorgeous Firebird. She escapes, but leaves him a single, special feather; if he's ever in trouble, he can use the feather to ask for her help. Then Prince Ivan comes across thirteen dancing princesses. A sorcerer named Kaschei has put them under a spell so they'll stay with him forever.

The prince falls in love with one of the princesses and argues with Kaschei. The Firebird shows up after Prince Ivan calls her with the magical feather. She puts a spell on the sorcerer and his evil men, making them dance until they fall into a deep sleep. The Firebird leads the prince to an egg, which holds Kaschei's soul. When Prince Ivan cracks open the egg, the princesses and everyone under the sorcerer's control are set free.

I had been promoted to soloist four years before. I was performing in *Don Quixote* as a flower girl, on tour in Tokyo when Kevin told me that I'd be learning the role of the Firebird. I was surprised to hear this directly from him. For most ballets, ABT posts a cast list, which is where we see who will be performing what roles throughout the year. The list includes featured roles and understudies.

About a month before the first show, the board is updated to let us know which dates we'll be performing. The company staff also sends out press releases to advertise who will be starring in the upcoming performances.

I figured I was probably going to understudy the role of the Firebird, rather than being cast in the principal role. Even so, I was excited to learn the new steps choreographed by Alexei Ratmansky.

Alexei's choreography veers more toward contemporary than classical. He'd included two solos and a *pas de deux*. The ballet would be performed by three casts, and each Firebird would have a special entrance of her own. For my entrance, I was to run as fast as I could across the stage and then stop, even while the music was still playing. I was supposed to be wild and powerful as the Firebird, and my posture displayed it. Instead of maintaining the long, clean lines of classical ballet, I twisted my neck at an angle to resemble a forest animal.

When teaching new steps, many choreographers only tell the dancers what they want us to do. But Alexei was different; he showed us the moves that had come from him, dancing along with us as we learned. I also enjoyed being able to learn directly from the creator. Classical ballets were choreographed hundreds of years ago, and it's impossible to know exactly what the creator wanted the dancer to convey. Alexei's steps were fresh and modern, but they weren't easy.

I was on a summer layoff from ABT while I learned the part of the Firebird. I was also part of a workshop with another company: the Dance Theatre of Harlem, which had started up once again after a break that had lasted nearly ten years. The company's new artistic director was Virginia

Johnson, a founding member and one of its longtime principal dancers. I loved being at the Dance Theatre of Harlem,
working on choreography with a roomful of dancers who
looked like me and believed in me.

We were on a break from the workshop when I read
the news.

Someone had posted an ABT press release to Twitter:
the cast list for *The Firebird*. ABT's guest principal dancer,
Natalia Osipova, would be playing the part in the first cast.

The second Firebird would be me. Misty Copeland. The
first black woman to dance the role for a prominent ballet
company.

Tears sprang to my eyes as I processed the news. I was
speechless.

"Is everything okay?" one of the other dancers asked. "Is
it your family?"

"No," I replied. "I've been cast as the Firebird."

I started crying. I was too happy to contain my emo-
tion. All the dancers in the workshop started crying with
me. They rushed to hug and congratulate me.

As a professional dancer, your fellow company members
play many roles in real life: rehearsal partners, competitors,
friends, and family. Many of my closest friends today are

those I met after I started dancing—from San Pedro to San Francisco, and in New York City. You learn to celebrate each other's successes and mourn the disappointments.

Several dancers at ABT congratulated me on being cast as the Firebird. But I was happy that I'd been at the Dance Theatre of Harlem when the news was announced. I was surrounded by black dancers who understood the importance of my casting. It was a historic moment for me, and all the hard work I'd put in at ABT over the past decade had been recognized in a big way. I had proved I was worthy of performing classical ballets. They knew how much that meant to me, and they were proud of what I'd accomplished. Just like I was proud whenever I saw black dancers breaking barriers.

I pushed myself harder than before, in classes and rehearsals. I lived and breathed the role of the Firebird, dancing for up to seven hours a day, six days a week for the next six months.

While I was preparing for the performance, word about my casting began to make the rounds. Many African American celebrities bought tickets to see me, the first black Firebird to perform with a major company. I received congratulatory phone calls from people I looked up to in the ballet world: Arthur Mitchell, Raven Wilkinson, Susan Fales-Hill. I should have been anxious, knowing that so many people I admired would be watching me, but I was too excited to let the nerves kick in.

My first performance of *The Firebird* wasn't at the Metropolitan Opera in New York. We performed the ballet for the first time in Orange County, California, at the Segerstrom Center for the Arts. My mother attended the performance. Even though he couldn't be there, Prince hosted a small party afterward for all my family and friends.

The ballet blogs were happy with my performance. Herman Cornejo played the male lead of Prince Ivan.

It was so good to see Herman in his solos, as he's looking amazing, one of the reviews said. *And Misty—her feet! her arms! her legs! her back!—was incredible. Both Herman and Misty moved through their backs, everything emanating from their center rather than a jumble of limbs being tossed about. They were fantastic apart and together, which is important for this ballet, especially as they aren't supposed to be a romantic couple.*

This cast can only get better, I'm sure, the piece went on. *I can't wait to hear others' impressions of them from the Met stage. Even though the Firebird is certainly different from*

Odette/Odile, Misty has the otherworldly drama and fluidity that makes me really want to see her in [Swan] Lake now. This ballet really shows [that] she's not just a technical firehouse . . . and I hope we get to see more of it soon!

The *L.A. Times* also praised our performance:

> Ratmansky's revised storyline and forward-backward movement idiom finally emerged clearly with second cast leads Misty Copeland and Herman Cornejo, a hypnotizing pair. Cornejo masterfully sustained tension and contained his energy, thus giving even more force to Copeland's abandoned, creaturely performance. With them, the audience's standing ovation was absolutely spontaneous.

I had been cast in an iconic role in a beautiful, inventive ballet. And I was shining like a star.

chapter 24

OUR PERFORMANCES OF *THE FIREBIRD* HAD
received great reviews, and we continued rehearsing hard for
our premiere on the Metropolitan Opera stage.

But my body wasn't so happy.

When I'd first joined the corps, I injured my lower back,
but I caught it early. I wasn't so lucky this time.

My left shin was hurting. I noticed about six months
before we were set to perform *The Firebird* at the Met. I'd
been pushing myself to the limit in rehearsals and performances on tour, and my leg was feeling the strain.

The pain hadn't gone away when I danced as the Firebird in
Orange County. In fact, there were a few times that my leg—
the leg that I turn on—hurt so badly I could barely breathe.

You're working out hard, practicing all day, I thought to myself. *Of course your leg is hurting.*

I didn't want to make things worse, so I no longer practiced my jumps during class. Instead, I would only execute *petite ellegros* and *grand ellegros* when we were rehearsing or performing.

I never told anyone that I was in such pain. I would be dancing the role of the Firebird, but I'd also been cast in *La Bayadère* as the second lead of Gamzatti. I didn't want someone to see I was injured and take the roles away from me.

This is for the little brown girls.

I couldn't let them down, not after I'd earned the historic role of the Firebird. I couldn't let myself down either.

I kept dancing.

The ballet mistress for *La Bayadère* was the celebrated Natalia Makarova, who had started her career as a prima ballerina with the Kirov Ballet in Russia and eventually became a principal dancer at ABT. Kevin thought I would be perfect for the part of Gamzatti, but Natalia would observe me for a few days to determine the final cast.

It was difficult, dancing under Natalia's gaze. She didn't think my curvy body was right for the role, and I felt it. I'd often want to break down in tears when we were in the studio, but I managed to hold them in so she wouldn't see me cry. I had to keep working toward my goals. I couldn't show weakness—not after everything I'd accomplished.

This is for the little brown girls.

I did perform the role of Gamzatti—once, before the Met premiere of *The Firebird*. I was still hurting, both physically and mentally, from Natalia's insistence that I wasn't talented enough to take on the part. But I succeeded, dancing better than I had in rehearsals. I had been ready for Gamzatti and I was ready for my New York debut as the Firebird.

The morning of *The Firebird* premiere, I woke at eight a.m. I shut off my beeping alarm and stretched my sore muscles.

Like most mornings, I ordered breakfast online: a black coffee and a blueberry muffin, which would be delivered by the deli on the corner. I'd have just enough time to eat and get ready before my day started with ballet class at ten thirty at the Metropolitan Opera House.

Even on one of the most important days of my career, I had to practice. The class was like nearly every other ballet class I've taken since I first started training. We started at the barre, pointing our toes into *tendu* and etching them in an arc along the floor as we executed *ronds de jambe*. Then we moved to the center to complete our class, building on the barre exercises, constantly strengthening our technique. All of that training would allow me to perform my best that evening in *The Firebird*.

I didn't jump in class. My leg was still hurting, and I wanted to save my strength for the performance.

We had a dress rehearsal at noon, to confirm that we were familiar with the stage. I made sure to know where I needed to be at all times. Otherwise, I could run into one of the corps members or mess up the timing with my *pas de deux* partner.

Then I had a private rehearsal with Alexei, the choreographer of *The Firebird*. We'd worked on the steps for months, but he still had small changes—even on the day of the first show. We went through my solos one last time to be sure I was perfectly in step at all times.

Beat one. *On my toes.*

Beat two. *Dart to the right.*

Beat three. *Bound through the air.*

Later, when I was leaving the Met to rest before the performance, my face was immediately warmed by the sun, a welcome change after being inside the dark, cool theater all day. I gazed out at the street, taking in the familiar sights and sounds of the city: honking cabs and meandering tourists and longtime city dwellers making their way along the sidewalks.

Then I turned to look up at the building behind me.

There, advertising our show on a twenty-four-foot banner, was a picture of me—Misty Copeland—standing *en pointe* with the poise, grace, and strength of a leading ballerina. I'd seen the banner when it had first gone up, but I still got emotional when I looked at it. I couldn't hold back the tears that sprang into my eyes. I'd been in New York City for more than a decade and this was the first time I'd ever seen a black woman's face on the front of the Met.

chapter 25

WHEN I RETURNED TO THE MET FOR THE
performance a few hours later, I was in undeniable pain.

I sat in my gorgeous crimson and gold costume in the
dressing room, surrounded by chocolates and photographs
and dozens of bouquets of roses and orchids. I had received
countless well wishes from friends and family and ballet lov-
ers through cards, texts, e-mails, and tweets.

In the hair and makeup chair, I was transformed. The
makeup artist made my face shimmer with sparkling red glit-
ter. My false eyelashes were a dazzling red color, and crimson
spirals were painted onto my skin, swirling out from the cor-
ners of my eyes. The costume was completed with a stunning
headpiece made to look like red and gold feathers.

Company members called out to me before I went on:
"Good luck, Misty!"

"Enjoy it!"

I was grateful for their words of encouragement, but I wasn't sure they knew how much pressure I felt. To represent not just ABT and Misty Copeland, but to show everyone that black women can succeed in ballet. That brown-skinned girls belong in ballet classes, schools, summer intensives, and major companies. That we have the talent and drive to make it to the top.

This is for the little brown girls.

I stretched and flexed my muscles in the lounge of the dressing room. I looked at myself in the mirror. *This is it. This is my moment*, I thought. But in that same moment, I thought about the pain. And I worried. *How can I dance if I can barely walk?*

I knew, deep down, that it would be the last night I took the stage for a long time.

My lower leg was aching, but I had to go out to the stage. Prove that this little girl from San Pedro, who had been promoted to soloist at the best ballet company in the world, deserved to be dancing in this principal role at the Met. I had been nineteen years old when I first stood on that stage. A new member of ABT's corps de ballet, dreaming of the day I would pirouette across the stage as a principal.

Kevin McKenzie was standing with the ABT staff behind the curtain. They wished me good luck before the performance began. Out in the theater, I'd never seen such a big crowd. Some of the most famous and accomplished members of the black American community and dance world were present: Arthur Mitchell, Debra Lee, Star Jones, Nelson George. They were all there to see me.

Prince Ivan appeared onstage, followed by a flock of "Firebirds" dressed in red and gold costumes that resembled mine. The orchestra started up the music and the lights clicked into place. My lower leg was in so much pain, but I knew I had to work through it. I couldn't disappoint all the people who had come to watch me, the first black Firebird in a major company production. I couldn't disappoint all the budding ballerinas who longed to see someone like them dancing onstage in a starring role.

This is for the little brown girls.

For the next hour and a half, I forgot about the pain. I put every ounce of my passion for ballet into the performance, into each *jeté*, *fouetté*, and *piqué* turn. And though they weren't with me onstage, I felt the presence of my biggest supporters.

This is a brisé, said the nurturing Lola de Ávila.

"You are God's child," said Cindy, always believing in me.

"Misty, you belong on the stage," Mommy encouraged after my talent show performance when I was five years old.

The audience loved the performance so much that sometimes I couldn't even hear the music over their applause.

At the end of the show, the theater was filled with exuberant clapping. I got a standing ovation and received a bouquet of flowers. Among all the commotion, I heard some people shouting "Bravo!" And later, I heard that a few audience members had been moved to tears as I'd danced.

Afterward, ABT had a party with friends and family to celebrate Kevin McKenzie. He'd been the company's artistic director for twenty years. But the celebration didn't stop there. I received so much positive feedback and encouragement from mentors, the media, and fans.

You have made it, my idol Raven Wilkinson wrote to me. *You are officially a ballerina! You have proven yourself in such extreme roles as Gamzatti, then Firebird. I'm so proud of you. You have more than I ever did, but I can still see when someone is the real deal. You are the epitome of all a ballerina is.*

Debra Lee, the president of Black Entertainment Television, wrote about my performance: *There are but so many special moments in our lives and last night was indeed one of them. . . . What joy to watch Misty on that stage!! What pride to share in her amazing accomplishment and historic performance.*

The writer Veronica Chambers reached out as well. *Tonight, it was as if you handed each of us—young girls and big girls—a set of wings,* she said.

Natalia Makarova, the ballet mistress who had been skeptical during my rehearsals for *La Bayadère*, was quite pleased with my performance as Gamzatti. I recorded her praise in my diary:

Hearing the applause when the veil is removed from my head, I felt confident and in control. Kevin was pleased, Makarova was ecstatic. [She] said I rose to the occasion and did everything she has been asking for. Firebird was an incredible success. The night was huge and beyond me.

I was thrilled to receive such praise from people I respected and admired. And I was floored by the review of my *Firebird* performance in the *New Yorker* by Joan Acocella:

A Firebird has to be like a bird, but to move us she also has to be like a human being. That didn't happen until the second night, when the role passed from Osipova to Misty Copeland, an ABT soloist. Copeland is the only highly placed African American woman in ballet in the city. Now they should promote her for artistic reasons as well as political ones. She deserves it.

A few days after the performance, I had dinner with a table of friends and ballet luminaries that included Arthur Mitchell; Lorraine Graves, a former dancer; Robert Garland, resident choreographer at the Dance Theatre of Harlem; and my friend Vernon, who works at ABT.

Arthur had been incredibly supportive of my career over the years. He'd called me after my performances in both *La Bayadère* and *The Firebird* to say how proud he was of me. At the dinner, he told me I had arrived. I was a queen. I was a true *ballerina*.

"You are beautiful," Arthur said. "You have the lines, the technique, the body. You are classy and smart. You have the total package, which few have. You can have any role you desire. You have no limits."

I felt so special. So humbled. I tried to remember that I should enjoy these moments. Bask in the praise and kind words about how hard I had worked to hone my talent over the years.

But I needed to remind myself not to wallow in negativity either. Later that evening, after dinner, I read a critical review from a blogger who didn't like my performance as Gamzatti. They didn't think I had the skill or grace to be a principal dancer. They thought if ABT promoted me, the company would be doing so only to prove it was racially inclusive.

I felt terrible. It seemed that no matter how well I performed and how hard I trained, some people would never be happy. And I wondered how many people in the audience had agreed with this blogger.

But that sadness turned to anger. That was one blogger. One opinion. And I wasn't done striving to be promoted to principal. I would keep growing as a dancer, keep improving my technique. I would prove that I belonged, not just as a talented dancer but as a talented black woman. I would make them see that I had earned every moment of my time onstage, in the spotlight. And one day I would show them that I deserved to be a principal, dancing center stage in classical roles.

I also realized that if I were promoted, the negative

comments wouldn't stop. I'd be giving even more interviews, appearing in even more shows. The negativity would probably increase. So I had to cherish the special nights, the incredible moments. I had to keep working toward my dream.

I had no idea of the difficulties I would face in the coming months.

My first performance as the Firebird in New York was also my last for that year.

On June 17, 2012, I told ABT I couldn't finish out the season. My leg was hurting too badly from my injury. I'd dealt with several stress fractures since my first injury after I joined the company back in 2001. My flexible knees make it easier for me to injure myself when I'm *en pointe*.

I recalled when I first started training at the Lauridsen Ballet Centre, under Diane. She had put so much emphasis on making sure I properly executed the basic moves I'd already learned with Cindy. I'd been frustrated. I already knew what I was doing. But now I realize that she was trying to prevent me from this very type of injury. My body was so flexible—could imitate any move I saw, no matter how extraordinary—that I was more likely to hurt myself than dancers who didn't bend so easily.

My previous injuries hadn't stopped me. I'd had several over the years, like every professional who dances for a living. We put so much pressure and strain on our bodies, it's usually only a matter of time. But this injury wasn't like the others.

I'd spent six months practicing and rehearsing for *La Bayadère* and *The Firebird*, and that whole time I'd been damaging my leg. Now my shinbone—the long bone below my knee—had six stress fractures.

I felt so defeated. I'd endured so much through my career from the start: struggling with the prejudice and racism that runs rampant in the ballet world, fighting to be cast in the classical roles I'd dreamed of, maintaining my confidence even through the negative whispers and comments. I'd made history as the first black woman to be promoted to soloist at ABT in almost twenty years and then as the first from a major company to dance the lead role in *The Firebird*.

I'd excelled in my roles as Gamzatti and the Firebird, and now I wouldn't be able to continue them throughout the season. I felt like everything I loved had been taken from me. I felt even worse when I looked at the cast list for the rest of the season. My name was noticeably absent, though I'd just recently won starring roles.

This wasn't going to be an easy surgery, though. I would

need time to recover to make sure I didn't injure myself again. The worst possible thing would be to ignore my body's pain until I could no longer dance at all.

I wrote about my disappointment in my journal:

I just don't know how much stronger I can be and for how much longer. I'm grateful for what I do have, but sad that it's not enough. . . . When will it ever be easy?

chapter 26

I HAD SURGERY ON OCTOBER 10, 2012. THE
next seven months were spent healing so I could return to
performing.

I spent those months keeping up my strength with private floor barre classes. Developed by Boris Kniaseff, the technique is called *barre à terre*. My instructor, Marjorie Liebert, helped me so much during my rehab. She was a ray of positivity when I felt so dejected. I didn't feel like myself. Ballet had defined me for so long that I didn't know who I was when I wasn't dancing. But with Marjorie's help, I began to learn about how the injury had affected me and what I could do to try to prevent it in the future.

Since I couldn't walk, the classes took place in my

Upper West Side apartment. I'd just had my cast removed. Marjorie guided me through the ballet barre while I was lying on my back, stomach, and side. I had such limited use of my body, but I was able to practice my *port de bras*, the carriage of the arms. So much of ballet is focused on the feet, but the arms are an extremely important part of telling a story through dance.

I slipped on my pointe shoes a month after my surgery. I couldn't stand *en pointe*, but the muscles in my feet needed the familiarity of the shoes for when I'd eventually step back onstage. Cindy had been so pleased and proud that I'd been able to dance *en pointe* so quickly after starting ballet. Now I wished it were so easy to step back into those shoes and up to the barre.

Marjorie helped me work through my frustration. She said my injury wouldn't last forever. She told me I couldn't give up on my dreams. I had to keep believing in myself and my abilities, even while I was temporarily unable to dance.

Every three weeks I visited the doctor for new X-rays. I had weekly appointments with an acupuncturist and a masseuse. I also attended classes called Gyrotonics, which helped me stretch and strengthen my body with machines. This allowed me to practice jumps while lying on the floor;

that way I wouldn't have to risk reinjuring myself by being on my feet.

I was cleared by my surgeon to begin rehearsing with ABT five months after my operation. Two months after that I returned to the stage in my first performance: *Don Quixote.* I danced as the Queen of the Dryads. A principal role.

I knew it was too soon. I wasn't able to dance to my best ability. Some critics agreed.

"Misty Copeland has absolutely no jump," one said.

I've always prided myself on my jumps. But I hadn't fully returned to leaping in class and rehearsal. I'd saved my *grand jetés* for the show, and I didn't execute them as well as I—or others—were used to.

It was difficult to heal in front of so many watchful eyes. Some people criticizing my performance didn't know about my injury. Others knew but didn't care. I didn't like knowing that several people were seeing me perform for the first time so soon after my injury. I knew I was capable of so much more than what I was able to give in those performances.

I didn't want to miss out, though. I needed to take time for my shinbone to heal, but I also worried that if I sat out too long from ABT, I would no longer be cast in the principal roles I'd dreamed of for so long.

As hard as it was to read the negative reviews, I know that critique is often what propels me forward. There will always be people out there who just don't like how I dance. I can't change that. But if several people have the same criticism, I start to pay attention. And if Kevin McKenzie, my artistic director, has the same issue, I know it's a part of my technique that I need to work on. Once, I read a quote from Kevin that said that my arms were weak compared to the ability of my legs and feet. I didn't like knowing he felt that way. But after that, I worked to improve my *port de bras*. And now I think my arms are one of my greatest strengths.

It's a bit easier to ignore the negative feedback when I know I've worked on that particular movement. As long as I'm continuing to grow and learn and hone my technique, I can stay confident in my abilities. Not everyone will love what I do, and that's okay. In the meantime, I will keep striving to be the best ballerina I can be. I will never reach perfection—no one ever truly can, ballerina or not—but I will keep working toward it as long as I am dancing.

Though I was injured and had to pull out of the season at the Met, I was given many wonderful opportunities before the surgery and after my recovery.

I was photographed by Gregg Delman for a ballet-focused calendar. Along with various athletes and artists, I filmed commercials for Diet Dr Pepper. I taught master classes for young dancers. I was also appointed an ambassador of the Boys & Girls Club, my refuge after school so many years ago in San Pedro.

Some people don't like that I share ballet with the masses. They don't believe ballet should be mainstream. But I've always wanted to share my love for dance with those who haven't been exposed to it. I realize how lucky I was to be taken under the wing of people like Liz Cantine and Cindy. They recognized my potential talent and helped me begin a life in the arts. I know not everyone will have the opportunities I've been given, and I believe everyone deserves the same chances I had. And I was able to bring that passion to ABT's Project Plié, which I helped establish in 2013. Through the program, ABT partners with the Boys & Girls Clubs of America to bring ballet to communities that don't have easy access to the arts. Kids learn about the history of dance, and the most talented ones receive scholarships to help with their training.

I've been reminded of how different I am since I first entered the ballet world. And now I'm using that difference for good—to remind people that coming from a low-income background should not stop anyone from pursuing their love of the arts. Of dance.

I also believe it's important to broaden the audience for ballet. I didn't see my first ballet until I was a teenager, and that's true for many children. However, according to studies, dance increases success in many areas of life because of the discipline and determination it requires. Everyone should have the opportunity to develop those skills. Change takes a long time, but I will keep working toward these goals, even if I don't see them achieved in my lifetime.

chapter 27

SO, WHAT'S NEXT?

That's the question I hear most often once people learn that I was the first African American dancer to be promoted to principal at ABT.

I've heard that question from journalists, fans, and friends. They're asking because they're excited for my future. But I usually just smile at their interest, shrug and reply, "Rehearsal."

My career has also led to so many other amazing opportunities. For example, I have become an ambassador and spokesperson for Seiko watches and Dannon Oikos Greek yogurt. I have a Barbie doll! How insane is that?

I have been able to dive into different genres of performing because of the incredible platform I have from these different brands that align with and understand me and what I stand for. I performed on Broadway in *On the Town*. I never imagined I would step outside of classical dance, but it made me grow in ways that every scary and new adventure has. If I never stepped outside of my comfort zone, I wouldn't be who I am or the artist that I am today. Broadway made me a better ballerina.

I've also had the opportunity to create my own dance-wear line called Égal Dance. This line means so much to me, as a dancer who has had a hard time finding dancewear that is really supportive. Especially for women who have larger busts, but also for any woman who wants to jump, run, and dance with comfort and ease.

I am also continuing to write books, which I really love. I never realized that from being so shy as a child, when my natural reaction was always to write, that I would actually share those words with the world. My next book is called *Ballerina Body*. I get to tell how I take care of my body, which allows me to dance and perform the way I do. What I eat, how I exercise, and how I keep my mind focused.

★ ★ ★ ★

I was twenty-four years old when I was promoted to soloist. Kevin had called me into his office to tell me after I'd
competed for the Erik Bruhn Prize. He'd told me I had to
keep it a secret for a while. ABT's spring season hadn't yet
ended, and he planned to announce all the promotions
at a company meeting. Then the news would go out in a
press release.

I was in one of the ABT studios when I learned I'd been
promoted to principal. I'd spent so many years of my life in
that room since 2000, when I'd become a member of the
Studio Company. Now, fifteen years later, I found out in
that very room that I had achieved my ultimate dream.

I was sitting in the studio before rehearsal when the
news was announced. Julie Kent, who had danced with
ABT for thirty years and just recently performed with the
company for the last time, filmed the whole thing. I didn't
know she'd caught such a special moment on video. I was
stunned when my promotion was announced. The next
several seconds moved in slow motion. Kevin said, "Misty,
take a bow." My dear friend Jennifer Whalen hugged me
and kissed me on the cheek. As soon as I pulled away from
her, I began to cry tears of joy.

I'd done it. For myself and for all the little brown girls.

I've achieved my nearly lifelong dream, but I'm still figuring things out. And I'm learning new things all the time. Like even though I felt so alone for so long at ABT, there were many people out there who related to me and my story. I had a difficult childhood, but others have similar experiences to share. That helps me make peace with the more challenging parts of my life, just knowing others out there connect with me on those levels.

As proud as I am of becoming the first black woman principal dancer at ABT, sometimes I wish the honor had gone to someone else. There were so many talented, hardworking black ballerinas who danced before I'd ever taken my first class, and I know so many of them were never given the respect or opportunities they deserved. Shortly before I was promoted, a travel magazine published an article about the profound impact Raven Wilkinson has had on my life and career. It is one of my favorite interviews I've ever done.

Fame has never been my end goal. I believe it's important to tear down the secrecy and exclusiveness surrounding ballet. I believe everyone should have access to the arts. And while I did want to make history with my promotion, I was most interested in showing that black women can excel in what has been thought of for centuries as a white profession.

I believe it's important to show young dancers that brown-skinned women with curves have the ability to break barriers. I want them to look at what I've accomplished and realize they can achieve this dream too. I often say that if there is space for a little brown girl from San Pedro in ballet, there is room for you, too.

I began rehearsing only a few minutes after my promotion was announced. I had to prepare for my upcoming performance as the Autumn Fairy in *Cinderella*. And I was back in class the next morning. I'd had the evening off to celebrate my accomplishment, but there was no time to rest.

I was different in the eyes of the ballet world now. I'd climbed my way to the top. I'd made history. Broken barriers.

But inside, I was still just Misty Copeland.

Working hard on my passion to be the best I could possibly be.

acknowledgments

I never thought that I would be so blessed as to be given the opportunity to share all that makes me *me*: my dreams, my struggles, and my hope to inspire many to dare to dream bigger than they can imagine.

I have to thank my family for the strength we have maintained throughout our lives. Erica, Doug, Chris, Lindsey, and Cameron: it was our belief in one another and ourselves that made it possible to beat and defy all odds. Thank you, Mom, for not giving up. Thank you, Daddy, for stepping into my life and raising me as your own. Cindy, Wolf, and Patrick: What can I say other than that I'm not sure where my life would be without our fateful meeting. Thank you for taking me into your home without judgment . . . just genuine love. Thank you for bringing me to ballet! I will forever be grateful. Thank you, Liz and Dick, my godparents. Thank you for not only being the catalysts to my career but for remaining a part of my life: for your guidance and love.

Boys & Girls Club of San Pedro! Boys & Girls Clubs of America! Everything you stand for is real, and it *works*. You change lives and started my future, and what a future it has become!

American Ballet Theatre: thank you for the endless belief and support in me. I'm proud to be an ABT baby. From the summer intensive to the Studio Company to a member of the main company! Thank you for helping to create an atmosphere where I felt capable of being a new mold for what a ballerina can be! To Susan, my second mommy, I can't say enough. Your mentorship changed my views and mind-set. You have set the bar high. Vicky! I think you were one of the first brown ballerinas I ever met. Thank you for taking the time to show me that I'm not alone, and for being an incredible example that my dreams are limitless. Diane, the short time spent training at the Lauridsen Ballet Centre was so vital to my training. Thank you for *never* taking it easy on me, for never treating me any differently from your other students, and for pushing me beyond what I thought my limits were. Raven, you gave me that second wind, inspiring me not to feel sorry for myself and my situation, but to fight for what I know is right. You remind me every day that life isn't easy, and therefore the fight in me is that much fiercer. Your perseverance is beyond admirable. You will always be that example of what a true ballerina is! Marjorie, I don't have to say it, because we both know it. We speak the same language, and your knowledge is endless. I admire and respect you, and I am grateful for the discoveries I have started to uncover within myself and my body because of you.

Gilda, where would I be without you? Vernon's introduction brought forth this magical collaboration that neither of us knew could reach these heights. And boy, do we have so much higher to go! Thank you for your incredible vision and for bringing it to life. You've brought ballet to a level I wasn't sure was possible. To the team at Touchstone/ Simon & Schuster, Megan Reid, and Steve Troha: Who would have thought . . . well, you guys did! And it's all happening. Thank you for the tremendous work and belief! Charisse, what a beautiful experience this has been, to sit in my living room and talk to a friend. This book has been far from work. It has been an exploration of myself, my past, and my future. Your words have brought it to life!

And last but not least, O. Our relationship has been more than I could have ever dreamed of it becoming. You have been my biggest fan, my voice of reason, and always good for a debate when that's needed. Thank you for being here always, and for helping me to believe that brown ballerinas could benefit from seeing and hearing my story and for encouraging me to be a mentor.